THE SINGING HEART:
A BOOK OF QUIET REFLECTIONS

THE SINGING HEART:
A BOOK OF QUIET REFLECTIONS

IVAN ILYIN

Translated by Alexandra Weber

ORTHODOX
CHRISTIAN
TRANSLATION
SOCIETY

Published in Russian as Поющее сердце
© The Publishing House of the Moscow Patriarchate
of the Russian Orthodox Church 2005

English Translation
© 2016 Orthodox Christian Translation Society
Memphis, Tennessee

Printed in the United States of America

Publishers Cataloging-in-Publication Data
Ilyin, Ivan (1883-1954)
Поющее сердце
The Singing Heart: A Book of Quiet Reflections
Ivan Ilyin; translated by
Alexandra Weber

ISBN-13: 978-0692546840

Cover art: Mariamni Plested, "Russian Scene"

ORTHODOX
CHRISTIAN
TRANSLATION
SOCIETY

In loving memory of Alice Causey Ewing

CONTENTS

Ivan Ilyin (1883–1954):
The Prophet of Faith and Love

There is only one true 'happiness' on earth – the singing of the
human heart. *If it sings, then a person has* almost *everything;*
almost, *because he still has to take care that his heart does not
grow disappointed in anything and does not fall silent.*
The Singing Heart, *Ivan Ilyin*

Born in central Moscow on March 28, 1883 into a noble, Orthodox,
and well-educated family, Ivan Alexandrovich Ilyin showed
his brilliance at high school, and in 1901, following in the footsteps
of his father, went on to study law at the University of Moscow. In
1906 he completed his studies in law and also philosophy, having
shown such an outstanding mind that he was preparing to become a
professor. In the same year, then aged 23, he married Natalia Vokach,
a graduate student who was close to him in spirit. His first writings
were published in 1910, and he and his wife then spent two years
in Germany, Italy, and France, where Ilyin studied at well-known
universities and met the Western philosophers of the age.

Returning to Russia after this, he taught and in 1918
received a professorship at the age of only 35. However, with the coup
d'état of February 1917 and the overthrow of the Tsar, he turned
from an academic into an active politician. He prophetically saw
the catastrophic nature of the situation and of Bolshevism. When
the Bolsheviks seized power in October 1917, he denounced them
in article after lucid article. This led to his repeated arrests and
harassment by the regime. Arrested six times in all, in 1922 he was
exiled to Germany with a large group of 160 prominent intellectuals
on "the philosophers' steamer."

Now in exile, he continued to denounce the Bolsheviks in
his speeches and his writings, having seen through the revolutionaries

in ways that few outside the Russian Church could understand. In all his works he remained a monarchist and was loyal to Orthodox Russia, despite the anti-Russian regime temporarily in power there.

For eleven years Ivan Ilyin worked in Berlin as a professor at the Russian Scientific Institute. He kept in close contact with exiled Russians around Europe and became a leading ideologue of the future Russian national revival. In particular he was very close to the future Latvian Orthodox martyr, Archbishop John (Pommer) of Riga, who, recognizing Ilyin's gifts as a public speaker in over 200 public lectures between 1926 and 1933, wanted to ordain him. Moving around Germany, France, Switzerland, Czechoslovakia, Yugoslavia, Austria, and Latvia, Ilyin spoke on Russian cultural, philosophical, and religious themes in Russian, French and German, and was also a member of the School of Slavonic Studies in London.

One of his greatest works was on resisting evil by force, and here he opposed Tolstoy and the Paris School of gnostics, philosophers, and artists including Nikolai Berdyaev. His writings were published everywhere in the Russian Orthodox émigré press. In the 1930s he worked with young people and wrote extensively about Russia. Notably, his "Three Speeches about Russia" were full of yearning, anger, pain, and his ardent faith in Orthodox Russia. Ilyin also published in German, including the articles "What is the Message of the Martyrdom of the Church in Soviet Russia for Churches in the Rest of the World?" (1936), "The Martyrdom of the Church in Russia" (1937), "Christianity and Bolshevism" (1937), and "The Attack on the Eastern Church" (1937).

Ilyin's writings greatly displeased Adolf Hitler, whose regime had in 1934 already dismissed Ilyin from his post for refusing to praise Fascism. Finally, in 1938 Ilyin was forced to leave Nazi Germany, his writings and speeches being forbidden by the Nazis. With great difficulty and help from Sergei Rachmaninov and other friends, he took refuge near Zurich in Switzerland (where, ironically, Vladimir Lenin had once lived in exile). In August 1934 Ilyin had already written to his friend the great Russian émigré writer Ivan

Shmelev about his pain at feeling lonely and unneeded by his homeland. Now it was even worse. Yet again in Switzerland Ilyin began to write and speak in public, often under pseudonyms, doing what God had given him life and talent to do.

His work became more philosophical, more spiritual, less political, and he began to stand up for family and patriotic values. After World War II he published his *Axioms of Religious Experience* and three volumes of philosophical and literary prose, originally written in German. He also wrote much of an uncompleted book on monarchy, which had been thirty years in preparation. After his death a two-volume anthology of articles published since 1948, called *Our Tasks*, was also issued. This was about the future of Russia once it would be freed from Communist atheism. Here, one article entitled "What the Dismemberment of Russia Will Do to the World" (1950) was particularly prophetic.

He reposed on December 21, 1954. At his funeral Archimandrite Constantine Zaitsev said, prophetically, that Ilyin's name would not be forgotten. And today Ilyin is considered by a great many to be the voice of the faithful Russia, a spiritual leader, a teacher, a prophet, a visionary preacher. He is a "stone that was rejected" which has become "a headstone of the corner." His prophetic insights have been justified since the fall of Communism and the huge interest in his works in today's Russia. Ilyin, who died over sixty years ago, is the prophet of the new Orthodox Russia which is now being reborn and which can give the contemporary world a viable future, providing that it is given time to grow to fruition. Beyond the veil of this world his heart sang of the truths that the Holy Spirit inspired in him and he can make our hearts sing, too.

Ilyin was never downhearted and never despaired. His writings are full of a bright, deep faith. Though arguing that humanity has been morally blinded and is in the grip of materialism, irrationalism, and nihilism, Ilyin put forward that we can overcome this global moral crisis by returning to eternal moral values: faith,

love, freedom, conscience, motherland, and nation. Most importantly—
as Ilyin himself ever proved in life, thought, and work—we must
return to faith and love.

Archpriest Andrew Phillips (M.A. Oxon)
England, Lazarus Saturday, 4 April 2015

FOREWORD

About Reading

Every writer worries about how he will be read. Will his readers understand him? Will they see what he wanted to show them? Will they feel that which his heart has loved? Who will his readers be? So much depends on this... Most importantly, will they experience that desired spiritual meeting with themes distant yet near, for which the author secretly wrote his book?

The problem is that many readers have not mastered the art of reading. Their eyes run across the letters, "words launch themselves from the page at any moment,"[1] and every word "means" something; words and their meanings get tied together, and the reader imagines things "second-hand," nebulous, sometimes obscure, sometimes pleasantly transient; all of which are then quickly spirited away into the forgotten past... And this is called "reading:" mechanics without soul; entertainment without responsibility; an "innocent" diversion. In reality, it is a culture of superficiality and a flood of vulgarity.

No author wishes to be subjected to such "reading." We all dread such "readers." For true reading happens in a completely different way and has a completely different meaning.

How was this book born, how did it come to be?

---

[1] N.V. Gogol. "Not the words which he read, but the mere solace derived from the act of reading, was what especially pleased his mind; even though at any moment there might launch itself from the page some devil-sent word whereof he could make neither head nor tail." Gogol, N.V. Hogarth, D.J., trans. *Dead Souls* (The Project Gutenberg ebook, 2008).

After having lived, loved, suffered, and enjoyed, observed, thought, and desired, hoped and despaired, the desire grows in a person to impart all this to us, as something that is important for us all, that is imperative to see spiritually, experience, muse over, and make our own: in other words, as something meaningful about something important and precious. And so he begins to seek out true images, brightly profound thoughts, and precise words. This is not easy; he isn't always or immediately successful. A responsible writer nurtures his book for a long time: for years, and sometimes his entire life; he doesn't part with it night or day; he gives it his best strength, his inspired hours; he agonizes over its theme and then finds healing through writing it. He searches for truth, beauty, "precision,"[2] a true style, a true rhythm, all to be able to impart, without distorting them, the visions of his heart... And finally, the work is ready. A final review with a strict, sharp eye, the final corrections—and the book breaks away and departs to the reader, one who is unknown, distant, perhaps frivolous and inconstant as spring,[3] perhaps virulently critical. It departs without him, the author. He excludes himself and leaves the reader with his book alone.

And so we, the readers, take to reading this book. Before us lies the accumulation of feelings, discoveries, ideas, images, imparted desires, directions, appeals, proofs—a spiritual tapestry, all of which is given to us hidden, encoded. It is locked beneath those black, lifeless hooks, those commonplace, overused words, those easily accessible images, those abstract concepts. The book's life, brightness, strength, meaning, spirit—all of this must be drawn out *by the reader himself.* He must recreate within himself everything that the author has created. And if he cannot, will not, or does not want to do this, no one else will do it *for him*; his reading will be in vain and the book will go over his head. It is generally accepted that reading is

---

[2] A.S. Pushkin. "Precision and brevity are the prime qualities of prose." Pushkin, A.S. Debreczeny, P., trans. *Complete Prose Fiction* (Stanford University Press, 1990).
[3] *Translator's note:* Here Ilyin creates a word, "легко-веснокапризному," out of three words: frivolous, inconstant, and spring.

obtainable to any literate person. Unfortunately, this is not the case. Why?

It is because the true reader gives a book his free attention, his entire spiritual capability, and his ability to evoke within himself that faithful spiritual state essential for understanding *this* book. True reading does not consist of running printed words through the consciousness; it requires a focused attention and a firm desire to truly hear the voice of the author. Mere intellect and an empty imagination is not enough for reading. It is necessary to *feel with the heart and contemplate from the heart.* One must relive passion through passionate emotion; one must experience drama and tragedy with an active will; in fine lyrical poetry, one must hear all the sighs, tremble with one's own tenderness, gaze into all the depths and distances; a great idea, however, must demand no more and no less than the *entire* person.

This means that the reader is called upon to faithfully recreate the spiritual and internal act of the writer within himself; to live through this act and trustingly give himself over to it. Only the reader and writer, after which all the vital and significant things that occupied and immersed the author will be revealed to the reader. True reading is in its own way an *artistic clairvoyance*, which is designed and able to recreate the spiritual visions of another person completely and faithfully—to live within them, to delight in them, and become enriched by them. The art of reading banishes loneliness, separation, distance, and age. It is a power of the spirit bringing letters to life, uncovering the prospect of images and the meaning behind words, filling the inner scope of the soul, contemplating the immaterial, identifying with unfamiliar or even deceased people, and, together with the author, artistically and intellectually perceiving the essence of our God-created world.

To read means *to seek and to find*: for the reader seeks out, in a way, a spiritual treasure hidden away by the writer, desiring to find it in its entirety and to adopt it for himself. This is the creative process; to reproduce is to create. It is a battle for a spiritual meeting;

it is an *independent union* with him who originally acquired and amassed the sought-for treasure. And to him who never desired or experienced this, it will always seem that the impossible is required of him.

The art of reading must be acquired and developed within oneself. Reading should be profound; it should become creative and meditative. Only then will we realize its spiritual value and soul-transfiguring power. Then we will understand what should and should not be read, for some reading deepens a man's soul and builds his character, while some reading corrupts and weakens him.

Through reading one can discover and determine a person. For each of us is *that which* we read; we are how we read. All of us unnoticeably become, through the things we take away from our reading, a bouquet of flowers assembled through the things we have read...

The book for which I am writing this foreword was nurtured in my heart, was written from my heart, and speaks of my heart's song; therefore it is impossible to understand through a heartless reading. But I believe that it will find its own readers, who will truly understand it and see that it was written for Russians about Russia.

I. FIRST GLIMMERS

Without Love (From a letter to my son)

And so, you think that it is possible to live without love, but with a strong will, a noble goal, justice, and angry battle with wrongdoers? You write: "It is better not to speak about love: there is *none* in people. It is better not to call people to love: who will awaken it in the callous heart?"

My dear one! You are both right and wrong. Gather, please, your impatient patience, and consider my thoughts on the matter.

It is impossible for a person to live without love, because it *develops independently in him and overpowers him.* It is given to us from God and from nature. We are not at liberty to dictate to our inner world, to remove certain spiritual strengths and then replace them with others, planting in their stead other abilities that are not characteristic of us. We can train ourselves, but we cannot break ourselves down and rebuild ourselves from scratch according to our own discretion. Examine the passage of a person's life. The child adapts to the mother—through needs, expectations, hopes, pleasures, consolation, solace, and gratitude—and when all this materializes in a first and most gentle of loves, his personal fate is determined. The child yearns for the father, awaits his greeting, help, protection, and guidance; he takes pleasure in his love and loves him in return; he is proud of him, imitates him, and feels his blood within himself. This blood will then speak for him his entire life; it ties him together with his brothers and sisters and all his kin. And when later he ignites with mature love for "her" (or, accordingly, she for "him"), then the task lies in transforming this awakening of nature into a true divine visitation, and to accept it as his fate. Furthermore, is it not essential for him to love his own children with that love which all his childish hopes awaited from his parents? How then can we do without love? With what can we replace it? What can fill that terrible emptiness that forms in its absence? A person *cannot* live without love because it is *the foremost discerning force in life.* Life is like an enormous current that flows endlessly in all directions, that crashes onto us and carries us with it. We cannot include in our lives everything that it carries; we cannot surrender ourselves to its whirling chaotic content. He who attempts this will use up all his strength and destroy himself: nothing will come out of him, for he will lose himself in complete assimilation. We must be selective and deny ourselves much for the sake of relatively little; this little we must welcome, guard, treasure, save, develop, and perfect, and with it build our identity. *Love* is the one discerning force on earth: it "prefers," "adopts," "grows attached to," treasures, cares for, seeks, and preserves loyalty. At the same time, the will is simply an instrument of love in life's doings. Will without love is empty, hard, harsh, violent, and most importantly, *indifferent to good and evil.* It will quickly transform life into a prison discipline commanded by depraved men. Many organizations built upon such principles already exist on this earth. May God protect us from them and from their influence... No, we cannot be without love: it is a great gift—*to see the ultimate good, choose it, and live it.* We have the essential and precious ability to say "yes," to adopt and begin a selfless service. How terrible is a person's life without this gift! What vulgarity, what a wasteland his life becomes!

A person cannot live without love also because it is *the foremost creative power in a person.*

For human creativity does not arise out of emptiness, nor does it take place within an arbitrary combination of elements, as many superficial people now think. No, we can only create after accepting the divinely created world, after entering it, incorporating ourselves into its wonderful framework, and becoming one with its mysterious paths and principles. But for this we need the entire force of love, the complete gift of artistic reincarnation that is bestowed on man. A person creates not out of emptiness; he creates *out of something already created*, out of things existent: he produces something new from within the framework of the nature of what he is given— something externally material and internally spiritual. The creating person must heed the depth of the world and break out into song from within it. He must learn to *contemplate with the heart*, see with love, emerge from his little personal shell into the bright expanses of God, and find in them something Great—kindred—belonging to all, to completely experience it and create things new out of things ancient, things unseen out of things pre-eternal. So it is in all the most important areas of human creativity, in the arts and sciences, in prayers and judicial life, in the society of people and in all culture. Culture without love is a dead, condemned, and hopeless matter. Everything great and ingenious that has been created by man was created out of a *contemplating and singing heart*.

A person *cannot* live without love because the most important and precious things in his life are revealed specifically *to the heart*. Only a contemplative love reveals an unfamiliar soul to us for faithful, profound communion and mutual understanding, friendship, and the upbringing of children. All of this is inaccessible to heartless people. Only a contemplating love reveals to a person his *homeland*, i.e., his spiritual connection with his native people, his sense of ethnic belonging, a haven for his soul and spirit on this earth. It is a joy to have a homeland, but it can only be obtained through love. Not by chance do hate-filled people—today's revolutionaries—turn out to be internationalists. They are dead to love, and deprived also of a homeland. Only a contemplating love reveals a person's admission to piety and God. Don't be surprised, my dear, at the impiety and faithlessness of the northern nations. They adopted from the

Roman Church a faithless religious act, beginning with free will and ending with rational thought; having accepted it, they neglected the heart and lost its contemplative nature. This is what predetermined the religious crisis that they are currently experiencing.

You dream of a strong will. This is good and essential. But it is a terrible and destructive thing if it does not spring from a contemplative heart. You want to serve a noble goal. This is excellent and true. But how will you see your goal if not with your contemplating heart? How will you recognize it, if not through the conscience of your heart? How will you stay faithful to it, if not through love? You want justice, and this is something we should all seek. But justice requires an artistic discernment in the perception of individual people, and only love is capable of this. Angry battle with wrongdoers can be inevitable, and an inability to conduct it can turn a man into a sentimental traitor. But this anger should be *founded on love*; it should be its very embodiment for the purpose of finding in it justification and measure.

That is why I said that you are both right and wrong.

Furthermore: I understand your suggestion that it is better not to speak about love. This is true: we must live it, not speak of it. But consider this: the public and mindless propaganda of hatred is spreading throughout the world, the cruel and unrelenting persecution of love has arisen in the world—attacks on the family, rejection of the homeland, suppression of faith and religion. The practical heartlessness of some has become wedded to the direct preaching of hatred in others. Callousness has found its apologists. Malice has become a doctrine. And this means that the hour has come to *begin speaking of love* and rise to its defense.

Yes, there is little love in people. They have excluded it from their cultural acts, from science, faith, art, ethics, politics, and education. And as a result, modern mankind has entered into a spiritual crisis unprecedented in its depth and scope. Seeing this, understanding this, it is essential that we ask ourselves: who will awaken love in the callous heart if it has not been awakened by the life and word of Christ, the Son of God? How can we take this upon ourselves, with our limited human strength?

But this doubt soon falls away if we listen to the voice of our heart's contemplation, assuring us that Christ is with us and within us...

No, my dear one! We cannot live without love. Without it we are doomed, along with our culture. In it lies our hope and our salvation. And how impatiently will I now await your letter confirming this!

About Fairness

Since time immemorial people have been speaking and writing about fairness, perhaps even since the very time that they began to speak and write. But until now the question has remained unanswered— what is fairness, and how can we achieve it in life? It is difficult for people to agree on the matter. They feel its practical importance in their own lives; they foresee consequences not advantageous to them; and for that reason, they argue like those with vested interest, uneasily and warily, lest they agree and lead to their own detriment— what then?

Every one of us desires fairness and asks that he be treated fairly; every person complains of all sorts of possible injustices inflicted on his person, and begins to interpret the idea of fairness in such a way that is obviously unfair to others. He becomes convinced that his interpretation is correct, and that he treats others "with complete fairness," but never will he admit that others are outraged at his "fairness" and feel mistreated and neglected. The narrower, poorer, and more violent people's lives become, the more acutely they will experience this—and the more difficult it will be for them to communicate and agree with one another. The result is that there is just as much "fairness" as there are unhappy people, and universal, true Fairness is impossible to find. All the same, strictly speaking, Fairness is the only thing worth discussing.

This means that interests and passions distort the greater question; the mind is not able to find a true answer and becomes overgrown with foolish and cunning preconceptions. False teachings arise out of these preconceptions; they lead to violence and revolution, and revolution brings only blood and suffering, in order to disenchant and sober those who are blinded by their passions. So entire generations of men live in preconceptions and languish in disillusionment, and so it is that the word "fairness" is sometimes met with a sarcastic smile and a sneer.

And yet none of this compromises or unsettles the noble old idea of fairness, and we must oppose as before any soulless exploitation of it, any class warfare, any revolutionary equalization. We can be confident that the future belongs to it. The task at hand is to faithfully achieve its essence.

The French Revolution of the eighteenth century hailed and distributed the harmful preconception that people are "equal" from birth or nature, and that subsequently everyone must be treated "equally." This preconception of natural equality is the main obstacle towards a resolution of our main problem, for the essence of fairness lies specifically in an *unequal approach to unequal people*.

If people were indeed equal, i.e., identical in body, soul, and spirit, then life would be terribly simple, and it would be extremely easy to achieve fairness. It would be enough to say simply: "an identical fate for identical people," or "equal parts of everything to all," and the matter would be decided. Then fairness could only be achieved mathematically and realized mechanically; everyone would be satisfied, for people would in reality be like identical atoms, like little balls rolling mechanically from place to place, indistinguishable in their similarity, internally and externally. What could be more naïve, simple, and vulgar than this theory? What superficiality— or rather total blindness—could lead people to such lifeless and harmful views? One hundred and fifty years have passed since the French Revolution. We might have hoped that this blind, materialistic preconception had seen its day. But now, suddenly, it is reappearing, winning over blind hearts, celebrating victory, and heaping a deluge of unhappiness on people's heads.

In reality, people are *unequal* from nature and *dissimilar* in body, soul, or spirit. They are beings born with different sexes; they are naturally various ages, with unequal strengths and varying degrees of health; they are given unique abilities and tendencies, unique appetites, gifts, and desires; they are so different from each other, both physically and spiritually, that it is completely impossible to find two identical people in the world. Born from dissimilar parents, of varying blood and heredity, raised in different countries, brought up in different ways, accustomed to various climates, educated differently, with differing habits and talents, people create differently and produce what is unequal and irregular. They are spiritually not the same: all of them are of a unique mind, unique kindness, dissimilar tastes, each with his own opinions and his own moral conscience. In a word, they are different in *every* sense. And fairness requires that people be treated according to their own unique qualities, without equating those who are unequal or granting unfounded preference. They cannot be appointed equal responsibilities: the old, the sick, women, and children are not liable for military service. They should not be given equal rights: children, the insane, and criminals do not participate in political elections.

We should not require the same of everyone: from the underage and mentally incompetent less is required; from those who are called to authority more strictness must be required, etc. And so he who lays aside preconceptions and dispassionately looks at life will soon be convinced that people are unequal from nature, unequal in their strengths and abilities, and unequal in their social circumstances; he will be convinced that justice cannot require the same approach towards unequal people; on the contrary, it requires *inequality for the unequal*, but such an inequality as would correspond to the true inequality of people.

This reveals the main difficulty of the matter. There are endless multitudes of people; they are all different. How can it be arranged so that each receives in life a fate that corresponds to his uniqueness? How is it possible to keep up with these countless singularities, to give "to each his own" (according to Roman law)? They are not the same; consequently, they cannot be treated in the same way, but only in agreement with their uniqueness... Otherwise, the result would be unfair.

And so fairness in no way requires equality. It requires an *inequality* based on the subject. Children should be sheltered and treasured; this gives him a variety of fair privileges. The weak must be pardoned. The tired deserve leniency. The weak-willed need more strictness. To the honest and sincere more trust should be given. The loose-lipped call for caution. From the gifted person, it is fair to require more. Heroes are worthy of honor, to which the non-hero should not lay claim. And in the same manner, in all things and forever...

For this reason fairness is the *art of inequality*. At its root lies close attention to human individuality and life differences. But at its root are also a living conscience and a living love toward man. There is an especial gift of fairness that is present in everyone. This gift presupposes in a person a *kind, loving heart*, one which does not want to increase the number of the wronged, suffering, and embittered in the world. This gift also presupposes a living watchfulness, a sharpened sensitivity towards human individuality, and the ability to feel and understand others. The fair man rejects a mechanical interpretation of people according to abstract characteristics. He is contemplative, intuitive. He wants to examine each person individually and reach the hidden depths of his soul.

That is why fairness is a *creative* undertaking: it contemplates life through the heart, captures the uniqueness of every person, and tries to evaluate him faithfully and deal with him objectively. It is attentive, careful, social; it observes a sense of moderation; it is prone to sympathy, to delicate condescension and forgiveness. It has much in common with tact. It is intimately connected to a sense of responsibility. It is in its own essence *loving*: it springs from the heart and is a living manifestation of love.

It is foolish to seek fairness in hatred, for hatred is envious; it does not lead to fairness, but to universal equalizing. It is foolish to seek justice in revolution, for revolution seethes with hatred and vengeance; it is blind, it is destructive, it is the enemy of just inequality, it does not honor "higher abilities."[4] On the other hand, justice is in itself one of the higher abilities of a person, and its purpose lies in recognizing and preserving higher abilities...

People will achieve fairness in their lives when everyone—or at least many—becomes its living artist and masters the art of *objective inequality*. And then a fair system will come together, not through the work of institutions of justice, but with the organic intuitive passing of objective judgment and objective treatment for the sake of an uninterrupted living flow of human individuality. Fairness is not a bird that needs to be caught and locked up in a cage. Fairness is not an abstract law for all situations and all people, for such a law equalizes but does not *objectify* (from the word "object") life. Fairness should not be dictated by formulas such as "once and for all," "for all people," "everywhere." For it is in fact not "once and for all," but an *active stream of individual modifications*. It is not "for all people," but for each person separately. It is not "everywhere," but lives in exceptions.

Fairness can be found neither in the form of general rules nor in government institutions. It is not a "system," but rather a living entity. It should be imagined in the form of a stream of *living and objective love for people*. Only such a love can resolve the problem: it will produce a living fairness, recreate everything in life and in people's relationships, and create a new objective inequality.

That is why the most important thing in life is not a fairness "established once and for all;" this is an illusion, a chimera, a

---

[4] F.M. Dostoevsky.

harmful and foolish utopia. The most important thing in life is a *living heart*, a sincere desire for creative fairness; and also a universal certainty that all people truly and sincerely want creative fairness and honestly seek it. And if this were true, then people would easily come to terms with the inescapable injustices of life—relative, temporary, or accidental—and would willingly excuse them with their selflessness. For each would know that a true, i.e., loving and artistic, fairness would be awaiting him.

His Hatred

How painful, almost unbearable, can be the feeling that "he hates me"… Such a feeling of helplessness takes hold of the soul. You try not to think about it, which is sometimes possible. But even if you are not contemplating it, throughout the spiritual realm you feel that stream, that current, of another person's repulsion, contempt, and ill will. You don't know what to do; you cannot completely forget; you carry this curse on your shoulders throughout your life.

Every person, whether he knows this or not, is a living, emanating, individual center. Every look, every word, every smile, every action of a person emits a unique energy of warmth and light into the universal spiritual realm, and this energy wants to act within him, wants to be welcomed and allowed into other people's souls; once recognized by them, it wants to call them to respond and join in a living current of positive, creative communion. And even when a man seems not to stand out in any respect, or is merely absent, we feel his energy; furthermore, the stronger, more defined, and more intense his energy, the more significant and unique is his spiritual identity.

We experience another person's antipathy for the first time when we feel that our life energy is not accepted by that person; we sense it being pushed back or stubbornly refused acceptance by him. This is already unpleasant and painful. It may bring out in us a sense of dismay, or even confusion. A strange feeling of failure or personal ineptitude, or even the irrelevance of our existence, arises in our soul; the desire for communion is cut off, our energy loses its will to radiate, we are at a loss for words, the spring is taken out of our step, and our heart wants to withdraw. Withdrawn and unsocial people often inspire this feeling in open and social people even when there is no antipathy in them worth mentioning. But once antipathy is born it can grow to animosity, harden into repulsion, and deepen into hatred; this can happen whether or not we have done something concrete to deserve that hatred…

He who sees eyes that burn with hatred will never forget them. They speak of a personal malice and forebode misfortune, and he who sees them and feels himself to be the focus of this energy does not know what to do. A ray of hatred is indeed a ray, for it burns and sparks; it is loaded with energy, it is directed from one spiritual center to another. But a hateful center burns with black fire, and its rays are dark and terrible; their energy is not life-giving, as in love, but deadly and destructive. In its wake is felt the stifled convulsion of the soul—a torturous enmity that wants to inflict pain on another person and already carries it along with itself. And when you try to grasp what it is that so torments the hater, you are filled with horror at the realization that he dreams of seeing you destroyed by pain and is tortured by the fact that this has not yet occurred. I look at those hating eyes and see that "he" despises me; "he" rejects my life's energy with a scornful repulsion; "he" has drawn a line of separation between us and considers this line the sign of a permanent rift: he is one side of the line, filled with implacable enmity, and I am on the other side, insignificant, detestable, hated, eternally undefeated; an abyss stands between us. Having retreated into the corner of his hatred, he has become cruel and blind, and thus he responds to any signs of life from my direction with a murderous "no." This "no" has permeated all the energy that he directs toward me, which means that he does not accept my energy and cannot forgive or bear my existence in any way. If he could, he would incinerate me with his glance. He is possessed by the almost maniacal idea of my extermination: I am condemned, completely and eternally, and I don't have a right to live. As Lermontov wrote: "There isn't enough room on this earth for the both of us...."[5] In general and in every sense, it is a spiritual wound, a deformity, a tragedy...

How did this happen? Why? What did I do to deserve this hatred? And what should I do now? How can I be freed of this numbing curse, foreboding misfortune for me and threatening me with premeditated destruction? Can I stubbornly defy it, pass it by, attempt to forget this black malice? Do I have the right to do this? How can I be rid of the oppressive thought that my existence has brought out such spiritual illness in someone else, such spasms of revulsion?

Yes, but on the other hand, is it even possible to control another person's feelings? Is it possible to reach into the soul of your antagonist and calm or transform his hatred? And even if it were possible, where would you begin? How would you find enough strength and spiritual skill to do this?

When in life I encounter someone with real hatred for me, I first experience a sense of profound unhappiness, then dismay and a feeling of helplessness, after which I feel a firm desire to leave my antagonist, disappear from his sight, never again to meet him or know anything about him. If I manage to do that I feel calm again, but soon afterwards I notice that a depression and heaviness has remained in my soul, for the black rays of his hatred are still reaching me, piercing me through the vastness of the universal realm. Then I unwillingly begin to see inside his hate-filled soul and I see myself in its black rays—their object and victim. It is difficult to bear this for long. His hatred is not only *his* unhappiness, but also *mine*, just like an unhappy love brings unhappiness not only to the lover, but also to the beloved. His hatred causes suffering not only for himself, the hater, but also for me, the hated. He is already brought low by his

_____

[5] M.I. Lermontov. *A Hero of Our Time.*

condition; his human dignity has already suffered from his hatred; now this indignity must claim me also. But I cannot agree to this. I must take on this problem, make sense of it, conquer it, and try to transform and ennoble his sick passion. A wound has formed in the spiritual ether of the world; I must heal and tend it.

We cannot, of course, control other people's feelings; truly, it is not at all simple to find the true path and the spiritual strength required to solve this formidable task… But I know one thing for certain: this dark fire must be extinguished. He must forgive me and make peace with me. He must not only "grant me life" and come to terms with my existence; he must feel *happiness* because I live on this earth, and give me the chance to be happy for *his* existence. For, according to the great Orthodox man of wisdom Seraphim of Sarov, "Man is man's greatest joy"…

First and foremost, I must learn and establish how—and why—I deserve this hatred. How could his potential love for me have been transformed into repulsion, and his healthy respect for me into contempt? We are all born for mutual love and designed to have mutual respect for one another. Do I bear any of the blame for the fact that we are now both suffering—he the hater, and I the hated? Perhaps I unwittingly grazed an old, still-unhealed wound in his heart, causing all the accumulated legacy of his past, his previous sorrows and unforgiven wrongs, to collapse onto my own head. In such a case only compassion can help—a loving understanding of his soul. But perhaps without noticing I somehow infected him with my own hidden hatred, which has lived forgotten within me and emanated from me without my knowing it. In that case I must first cleanse my own soul and transform the traces of my forgotten hatred into love. And even if my share of the blame is completely insignificant and unpremeditated, I must start by accepting and eliminating it, even though this would compel me—with sincerity and love—to obtain forgiveness from him.

Secondly, I must forgive him his hatred. I should not, I dare not, respond to his dark rays with similar dark rays of contempt and repulsion. I should not avoid meeting him; I do not have the right to run away. I should meet his hatred face to face and give it a spiritually true answer with my heart and will. From this point on, I will respond to the ray of his hatred with a white beam—bright, humble, kind, forgiving, and seeking forgiveness, similar to that with which Prince Myshkin met the dark ray of Parfion Rogozhin. My beam should tell him: "Brother, forgive me; I have already forgiven everything and responded with love; please accept my existence in the same way that I accept your existence—with love." Indeed, with love, for to forgive is not only not to seek revenge, not only to heal the wound, but also to love the forgiven.

Two people are tied to each other with two threads: one from *him* to *me* and one from *me* to *him*. His hatred breaks the first thread. If it breaks, then we both suffer: *he* because his heart has convulsively shrunk back and hardened, and *I* because I must watch how tormented he is because of me; and also because I, despised by him, suffer because of him. There is only one way the situation can be saved. I must hold onto the second thread—leading from me to him—strengthening it and thus restoring the first thread. There is no other way. I must convince him of the fact that I am not returning his hatred with hatred; that I do not lay to his account his malice and animosity; that I recognize my possible fault and am trying to eliminate it and redeem myself; that I understand him, suffer together with him, and am ready to approach him with love; and, most importantly, that there is enough of my spiritual love to bear the weight and heat of his hatred, to meet it spiritually, and to attempt to transform it. I must treat my antagonist the way a gravely ill person is treated and not subject him to new, added suffering. Through my energy I must send him understanding, forgiveness, and love until he restores the broken thread leading back to me.

This will probably be difficult to do; his hatred will most likely prove stubborn, and will not want to be transformed or put to rest so soon. But I will be persistent and keep my faith in victory; it is my guarantee of success. Hatred is healed by love and only love. A ray of true love pacifies wild animals. This is what the lives of the saints tell us—it is not a fantasy or a legend of the faithful. The energy of love succeeds by pacifying and disarming; the force of malice is dissipated; the malicious instinct is lost: it gives way and is drawn into an atmosphere of peace and harmony. These are not empty words. Love calms tempests and preserves peace in the universal spiritual realm; even the gates of hell do not stand in the way of love.

If at some point this does take place, his hatred will be transformed; the wound in the spiritual realm will heal and recover; we will both rejoice with the joy of deliverance and will hear, high above us, exaltation and celebration to the very seventh heaven, for God's thread of love is again one and whole in all creation.

My Guilt

No, I have not yet learned to recognize and bear my guilt. I need more courage and humility. But perhaps someday I will achieve this.

How painful and sometimes torturously difficult it can be to determine and accept your own guilt. Your soul begins to feel agonized and restless, then grows callous and refuses to see the truth. You want to immediately defend yourself, deny your guilt, lay the blame on someone else, and most importantly to prove not only to others, but also to yourself—yes, specifically to yourself—that "this has nothing to do with me, and I am entirely guiltless in the matter. Everyone around me is to blame; in the end the whole world is at fault, but not I. Friends and enemies, nature and man, parents and educators, an unfortunate concurrence of circumstances and difficult conditions, 'society' and 'influence,' heaven and hell, but not I! And this can be proven—it must be proven—because there can be no doubt of it."

Oh, this treacherous "need" for self-justification! It gives me away completely. This chasing after evidence...why do I need

31

it if I firmly and definitively believe that "it has nothing to do with me?" Who demands this evidence from me? Who suspects me, if not I myself? This only attests to the fact that in the depths of my soul I do consider myself guilty after all; a certain quiet voice secretly repeats this to me and leaves me no peace...

And then suddenly, influenced by these unexpected realizations, I stop fleeing my own guilt. My cowardly anxiety ends. I am ready to be reconciled with the thought of my guilt, to search out my guilt and accept my fault. This cowardice has already led many astray, causing difficult internal conflicts, quarrels with one's own self, a division of self. Some it has led as far as hallucination. But I am ready: let my accuser speak.

Yes, courage is needed in order to investigate your own wrong without seeking deliverance from it in flight. Humility is also needed. If you do not overestimate your own strength and qualities, if you do not consider yourself the "smartest" and "kindest" person, then you will always be ready to presuppose your own guilt. Why should you examine all your actions from their best and noblest side? What naiveté! Where did this need come from to present yourself— to yourself, and to others—as an all-seeing righteous man who never makes mistakes? Why do you idealize your intentions and find peace only when an unprecedented image of purity and greatness shines out in connection with your name? Which of us is entirely free from imperfect desires and intentions? Which of us is right from birth and holy from our mother's womb?

No, I still need to learn what it is to carry a share of the blame, how to identify it and bear it throughout my life. How can I learn this?

First of all I must recognize the fact that all people without exception, while they live on this earth, *share the common guilt of this world*: through desire and a lack of desire, but also through a lack of will, a cowardly disinclination from willful choices; action and inaction, but also half-heartedness or a Pilate-like "washing of the hands;" feelings and thoughts, but also a wooden apathy and dull indifference. We are implicit in the guilt of the entire world—both directly and through the medium of others who are injured or tainted by us, and through yet others who, unbeknownst to us, come under our negative influence. For all mankind lives as if within one *all-encompassing spiritual realm* that draws us into itself and binds us to each other. We breathe in and out with this shared spiritual air of existence; we send our "waves" or "emanations" out into this realm, even when we do not realize it or do not intend to do so; we accept it from other people's emanations, even when we don't know anything about it. Every evil thought, every hateful emotion, every malicious desire, invisibly poisons this spiritual air of the world and spreads ever farther within it. Likewise, every spark of pure love, every noble movement of will, every solitary and wordless prayer, every thought of heart and soul, emanates into this universal living environment and carries with it light, warmth, and purification. We consciously and subconsciously read in each other's eyes and facial features, hear in the sound and vibration of voices, see in gestures, gait, and handwriting, much that is sacred, undone, unsaid; having taken this in, we carry it within ourselves and give it in turn to others. Not without reason does Koshchei the Deathless brood over his wicked plans. Not in vain does Baba-Yaga[6] carry her malice in her mortar. Not without purpose or effect do satanists abandon themselves to their meditations. Yet the solitary prayer of Simeon the Stylite nobly and powerfully illumines the world. The unknown saints, through whose efforts cities and kingdoms are held together, form the true and real foundation of human life.

This is why there are no "guilty" or "guiltless" people. There are only those who *know* of their guilt, who are able to carry their own and the world's shared guilt, and those who, in their blindness, *don't know* of this, but try to imagine and present before others their own imaginary innocence.

---

[6] *Translator's note:* Koshchei the Deathless and Baba-Yaga are common villains in Russian fairy tales.

The first type of people have enough courage and humility not to close their eyes to their own guilt. They know the true condition of the world and their implicit connection to all people; they try to purify and render harmless the emanations sent in their direction. They try neither to poison nor to taint the spiritual air of the world—on the contrary, they give it light and warmth. They remember their own guilt and seek a true awareness of it, in order to put out its negative influence and not increase its weight. They think of their guilt calmly and worthily, without resorting to a pretense of exaggeration or drowning in trivialities. Their knowledge of self serves the world and is ever ready for this service. They are *bearers of the world's guilt*, purifying the world and strengthening its spiritual fabric.

The other type are eternal fugitives, hopelessly "saving themselves" from their guilt, for their guilt pursues them as in the ancient tale of the *Erinyes*.[7] They imagine that they are responsible only for the things they deliberately and intentionally committed in their external lives; they don't know anything about the encompassing worldly ether and their shared worldwide guilt, in which all threads have become intertwined into an inseparable whole. They seek peace in their imaginary innocence, which to them and for everyone else is completely unachievable. How cleverly and logically they think, how remarkable their power of judgment when they expose those around them, pointing out their faults, blaming them, and stigmatizing them. And all because it seems to them that they justify themselves in this way. But when the matter concerns them, they suddenly become nearsighted, naïve, and stupid. If only they knew how much they are harming themselves and the world! They rush to prove to themselves that they are "very good" and "completely innocent," that they don't need to change anything about themselves or seek improvement. Yet precisely because of this, the

---

[7] *Translator's note:* The Erinyes, or Furies, were goddesses of vengeance and revenge in Greek mythology.

emanations they send forth into the world remain uncontrolled and unpurified; the world's air, already tainted and ailing, again and again soaks in the poisons of vulgarity, hatred, and malice sent forth from them...

If I have seen all this and now understand it, I am on the right path. Each of us needs first of all to sweep and clean our own home. This is where I must begin.

And so I do not seek deliverance in flight. I accept my guilt and carry it from this day forward—calmly, honestly, and courageously. There will probably be difficult and painful hours, but this pain is purifying and beneficial. I will seek out and find my own fault not only in external actions, words, and deeds; I will search farther, deeper, and more intimately into the unexpressed and unspoken conditions of the soul, where begins my total isolation and where even self-awareness does not reach. I will search everywhere: where do I lack love and forgiveness; where do I forget about the universal expanse and the shared ether of the spirit; where do I cease to serve God and to do His work—or at least, where I am halfhearted in this service?

If at any point I perceive my fault, my remorse over it must become true suffering to the point of repentance and the readiness to redeem it, and most importantly, to the point of my decision to change from then on and act differently. A true *feeling of responsibility* thus takes root inside me and stands watch over every new action.

Examining my personal guilt, I discover and untangle a hundred different threads, connections, and relations with other people. The fabric of communal life slowly unfolds before my eyes; I slowly become accustomed to absorbing and contemplating the universal expanse of spiritual life—and I begin to comprehend that I do indeed "send out" to and in turn "receive" from this shared atmosphere. This teaches me to faithfully measure my share of guilt without stumbling under its tangible weight. It is a harsh but

valuable schooling. Every step represents for me a stair leading to
the strengthening of my spirit and true nature. Without falling
into confusion or despair, I see my entire life as a chain of guilty
actions and states of being—and I draw from this more courage and
humility.

As I achieve this, I receive the right to explore the question
of the guilt of other people—not in order to expose them or judge
them, which I desire to do less and less, but in order to experience
their life situation and spiritual condition in such a way that I could
envision myself in the place of the guilty person in every instance,
and imagine that *his* guilt was *mine*. This considerably increases and
deepens my experience of guilt, and I slowly learn to carry not only
my share of the blame, but also that of other people, to carry it, i.e.
to conquer it, in my spirit and through love.

However, in reality, I still have very far to go... I don't know
if I will ever master this art. Perhaps, perhaps not... But of one thing
I am certain: this is the right path.

About Friendship

Every one of us experiences times in life when our innate and natural
solitude suddenly begins to seem heavy and bitter. We feel helpless
and abandoned by everyone, we search for a friend, but there are
none to be found... And then we ask ourselves, in amazement and
confusion, how it could be that for my entire life I loved, desired,
fought, suffered and, most importantly, served a great goal, but
found no sympathy, compassion, or friend? Why has no union of
ideas, mutual trust, or shared love tied me to anyone in a living unity
of spirit, strength, and support?

At that point the desire awakens in us to know how the
lives of other people unfold: do they find true friends, or not? How
did people live before us? Can it be that our time, in particular, is
witnessing the loss of friendship? Sometimes it seems that modern
man is decidedly not created for friendship, nor is he capable of it...

In the end, one is invariably led to the basic questions: what is true friendship, what comprises it, and on what is it founded?

Naturally, people often "like" each other and "keep company" with each other, even today. But my God, how meager this is, how superficial and shallow! It only means that their time spent together is "pleasant" and "amusing" to them, that they can "please" each other… If they discover an affinity in inclinations and tastes; if they successfully avoid annoying each other with their rough edges, evading any sharp corners and keeping silent about any conflicting opinions; if both know how to listen to each other's chatter with an amiable appearance, lightly flatter each other, and oblige each other a little—that is enough. A so-called "friendship" is formed between people, which is in essence founded on external conventions, slippery-smooth "manners," empty pleasantries, and hidden calculations. Some friendships are founded on a shared love of gossip or a mutual outpouring of complaints. But there are also "friendships" of flattery, "friendships" of vanity, "friendships" of patronage, "friendships" of slander, "friendships" of preference, and "friendships" of co-alcoholism. Sometimes one gives, the other takes—and both consider each other "friends." One hand washes the other: people manage their business and affairs together, not trusting each other too much and yet thinking that they have "become friends." But "friendship" is also a name given to a passing fancy between a man and a woman who hold no claim to each other, or sometimes it is a romantic passion that occasionally separates people once and forever. All these imaginary "friendships" boil down to the fact that people who are mutual strangers, or even completely unlike one another, cross paths and temporarily ease their lives through shallow and self-interested contact. They don't see, don't know, don't love each other, and often their "friendship" falls apart so quickly and disappears so completely that it is difficult to say whether or not they were previously even acquainted.

Throughout life, people bump into each other and bounce away from each other like wooden balls. A mysterious fate whirls them about like the world's dust and carries them through life's expanse into an unknown distance, and they act out the comedy of "friendship" within the tragedy of universal loneliness... For without a living love, people are more like lifeless ashes.

However, true friendship breaks through this loneliness, conquers it, and frees the person for the sake of a living and creative love. *True friendship...*if only we knew how it formed and developed! If only people knew how to preserve and strengthen it...

There is only one force in this world capable of conquering the loneliness of man, and that force is *love*. There is only one possible way of emerging from the dust of life and resisting its whirlwind, and that is a *spiritual life*. And so true friendship is *a spiritual love* uniting people, and spiritual love is the *living flame of God*. He who does not know the flame of God and has never experienced it will not understand true friendship, nor will he be able to recreate it, nor will he ever understand loyalty or true sacrifice. That is why only *people of the spirit* are capable of true friendship.

There is no true friendship without love, because love is what unites people. True friendship is a *voluntary union*; within it a person is at the same time free and connected. This connection does not interrupt or lessen freedom; rather, it brings it to life, and this freedom, finding life in unity, connects person to person in spirit. The strongest union in life is a voluntary union: if God is in its midst, if its members are brought together through God, and if it is strengthened before the face of God. This is why a voluntary, spiritual friendship lies at the root of every true marriage and healthy family. True friendship, as well as true marriage, is forged in heaven and never undone on earth.

If somewhere on earth we see true loyalty and true sacrifice, we can accept with confidence that they arose from a true spiritual closeness. Friendship is strictly unique to people of the spirit; it is their gift, their inheritance, their way of life. People without heart and without spirit are incapable of friendship: their cold, self-profiting "unions" always remain conditional and prone to betrayal, while their calculating and artful alliances exist on the same level as market trading and career making. A true union of people is possible *only within the emanation of God*, in spirit and in love.

The real person carries in his heart a certain hidden heat, as if a secretly burning coal dwelt inside him. It so happens that very few people know of this coal, for its flames are rarely discovered in daily life. But its light illuminates even an enclosed space, and its sparks reach out into the universal realm of life. And so true friendship arises from these sparks. If you have ever seen a speck of radium, you will never forget this miracle of God. In a small enclosed space, in the darkness, behind a magnifying glass, you can see a tiny solid from which little nimble sparks fly out in all directions and quickly disappear into the darkness. If a light turn of the screw lessens the grip of the tweezers holding this speck of dust, the sparks begin to fly out generously and happily; if the grip tightens, the sparks fly out thinly and carefully. Scientists assure us that the radial charge of this speck will be active for at least two thousand years…

The human spirit similarly lives and sparks; in this manner it emits its sparks into the world's expanse. From these sparks true friendship is fashioned.

There are people for whom the word "spirit" is not an empty sound or a dead concept: they know that life is filled with God's flowers and is brightened and enriched by them; they know that man is given an internal eye capable of seeing and recognizing these flowers. They search for them, find them, rejoice in them, and love them with all their heart. Such people carry in their hearts the "charge" of the spirit and the "heat" of the soul. Their own spirits are like the specks of radium emitting sparks into the world's expanse. Within these sparks love flickers, and the strength of the divine essence so loved by them shines forth. And every spark seeks acceptance, acknowledgment, and response, for human love always demands understanding and reciprocation.

But a spirit's emitted spark can be accepted and comprehended only by an active and radiant spirit, by a heart that itself loves and radiates. A cold darkness consumes everything without a trace. A lifeless emptiness cannot give answer. Fire is drawn to fire, and light reaches for light. And when two fires meet, a new and mighty flame arises, which begins to grow and tries to create a new and living tapestry of fire.

True friendship begins where the emitted spark of the spirit comes into contact with a person's burning bush and is accepted by it. A returning spark follows in answer to the accepted one; this spark unites with the first and in turn inspires a new response. Thus begins an exchange of light. The sparks never disappear into the surrounding darkness. Each reaches its goal and ignites in turn. Whole sheaves of light blaze forth, the flames flare up, and the fire grows: freely given talents, creative perception, bright gratitude…and not a shade of envy. The spirit rejoices in its meek sincerity. It knows that it will encounter spiritual contemplation and an empathetic understanding. The heart keenly listens and happily anticipates the future. And the divine flame makes celebration throughout the world.

Yes, the human soul is lonely on earth and often suffers from this. It can feel abandoned and forgotten. But the human *spirit* will not accept loneliness. It is rooted in the Divine, lives for God's work, freely emits its sparks, and is undaunted by any walls. It doesn't believe that atomic disunity, or scattered multiplicity, is the sealed fate of human existence or the inevitable form of life; it doesn't believe that people are doomed to wander in lonely chaos, never to find each other; it doesn't believe in the victory of the "world's dust." Somewhere (we do not know where), sometime (we do not know when), in the great depth of God's plans and creative ideas, the spirit saw a certain vision: a single, all-encompassing sea of flame *rested in slumber* in a prophetic tranquility, exactly as it was envisioned by God from the very beginning, and it was summoned to *an awakened existence* in the future. The spirit beheld this vision—it had stepped into this novel state of the world's being in order to awaken in the form of a single isolated "little flame," and to enter into creative battle on earth for the cause of *a spiritually awakened unification* of the flaming masses. For human souls—the spiritual flames of God—are called upon to undergo an individualization and separation, and merge anew into a single, all-encompassing sea, only this time as spiritually-awakened fire…

Thus true friendship, like love—or more specifically, spiritual love—creates the initial core of this unity; someday, these little cores of spiritual fire will form one great and unified flame of God, a bright and joyful tapestry of God's Kingdom throughout the entire world…

That is why every spiritually active person seeks true friendship on this earth, and is happy if he manages to find and achieve this friendship. In this manner, he carries out the testament of his Maker and partakes in the fulfillment of His promise; he thus takes part in the renewal and transfiguration of this Divine world.

There are many people on earth who know nothing of true friendship, but nevertheless helplessly attempt to define it; not finding their way to it or knowing how to achieve it, they satisfy themselves with a worldly, passionate "love," most of the time drawing from it only disillusionment and despair. But precisely these types of people should discover and feel that they are destined for friendship, and that it is within their grasp. For the most feeble ray of noble desire or compassion—the careful and sensitive approach of one person to another; the smallest spark of spiritual exchange, whether through active discussion, art, mutual exploration, or contemplation; the effort to pray together to the one God with similar grievances—already constitutes a beginning, the seed of true friendship. A stairway is built from the first step; a song begins its melody with the first utterance… How tragic it is when a life is ended at the root, when the staircase breaks at the first step, when a song is cut off at the first sound!

For this reason every one of us should search for true friendship throughout our lives, to spiritually construct it and lovingly preserve it. Only then will we discover what comprises the bliss of true faithfulness and the natural ease of true sacrifice.

II. THE SCHOOL OF LIFE

The Soap Bubble

This blessed little orb lives for a moment, just one brief instant—and then it is gone… What a happy instant! What a bright moment! But it must be created and captured in order to be enjoyed properly; otherwise, it will disappear forever. Oh, what a light symbol of earthly life and human happiness!

You must approach this matter with a light step, quiet movements, and bated breath: you carefully choose a straw, unbent, virginal, with no internal crack; then, taking care not to crush it, you must cut one end and bend back its walls. Then you cautiously dip it into the murky, soapy liquid, allowing it to absorb it and drink to its heart's content. Better not to rush; most importantly, you must neither be nervous nor lose patience. You must forget everything; extinguish all thoughts and cares. Release all your tense muscles. Give yourself over to a weightless equilibrium of the soul: this is a game, after all… You must find the desire for playful beauty and come to peace ahead of time with the fact that it will be momentary and quick to vanish…

Now you carefully pull out the straw, without shaking it, and trusting it like a loyal helper; then take a good breath of air, filling your lungs… And quietly, quietly, with a thin, barely noticeable sigh, give the lightest little push towards the birth of beauty…

There it is, the desired little orb; it starts to expand and grow… Don't stop your flow of breath! You must lovingly continue the game. Gently treasure the newborn creation. Increase its size with your tender exhalation. Let it tremble with a barely noticeable rhythm at the end of your straw, let it expand and grow...

There! Isn't it beautiful? The finished formation has joyful hues, increasingly more vibrant and varying shades of color, while inside it there is a playful circling movement. The orb grows and grows; its internal movement spins faster and faster; it sways back and forth more and more. An entire world of beauty, complete and transparent...

And now the creation is complete. It desires to break away, to become independent and begin its joyful and daring flight through the air. You must stop your breath and pull the straw away from your lips. The surrounding air must be still! No sudden movements, not a breath, not a word! You must slip the straw to the side with a careful gesture and set the aerial sphere free...

Oh, the daringly light flight to meet its fate... Oh, the brief instant of careless rejoicing!

And suddenly, it is over! The happy creation has shattered in every direction in a fine mist.

No more! We must start from the beginning... What childishness! What is the point of this child's play? Yes, of course, it is "child's play"... But all the same, it is not only for a "child," and it is no mere "play." I must admit I play this game with great enjoyment and have learned much from it...

For pity's sake, what can you learn from a soap bubble?

* * *

Any beauty—even the smallest and most pointless, as well as every joyful moment in life—has great and surpassing value. These beauties wash away the soul's grief; they bring us the easy breath of life (even when they simply teach us to carefully breathe out air) and give us a little bit of happiness... We can be sure that *no light, joyful moment has ever gone to waste* in a person's life and, consequently, in the history of the world… You must not wait for light beauty or the moment of joy to appear on its own and declare itself; you must call it, create it, rush to welcome it… And for this any naïve, innocent game will do, even if it only involves a straw and some soap. So much that is light and beautiful is hidden in a game, springs to life from a game. Not in vain do games draw inspiration from art—any form of art, even the most serious and difficult…

Do not take the game away from a grown person; let him play and enjoy it. In the game he rests, becoming happier, gentler, kinder, more like a child. Through his free and innocent concentration on the game, a devoted and self-forgetful immersion, his soul can be healed.

However, moments of beauty visit us rarely and stay only briefly. They vanish just as easily as the soap bubble. We must capture them and surrender ourselves to them in order to enjoy them to the fullest. They are not usually subject to human whims; we cannot summon them by force. Beauty comes to us with a light tread, often unexpectedly, by chance, on its own initiative. It will come, bring us joy, and vanish, obedient to its own mysterious laws. We must study these laws, too, for it is possible to adopt them; we must enter into their living current, submitting ourselves to them without demanding their submission in return…

For this reason we must learn to *listen*: to listen to the nature of things with bated breath, to enter into nature's living current, to be one with its joy and the beauty of the world. That is why he who seeks living nature, gentle art, and joyful play must free himself internally and eliminate any tension; he must surrender himself to these things with a child's spontaneity, preserving a light equilibrium in the soul and enjoying the beauty of the living object.

There is a strict limit to our willful, premeditated desires. They must grow silent and fall away. Only then can a person's creative will learn submission: *obedience to nature* is the path to happiness and beauty. We are not above nature; it is wiser than we.

It is stronger, for since we ourselves are of nature, it is our master. We cannot dictate it; its living current should not be broken. He who blows against the wind or resists its direction will not succeed. An impulse should not be interrupted; an interrupted impulse is no longer an impulse, only a lack of force.

But before we can surrender ourselves to a playful impulse or attempt the creation of new beauty, we must develop *trust* in our own selves. We must silence any objections or secondary considerations; we must give ourselves over immediately without watching over ourselves, or interrupting ourselves, or trying to be clever, or rendering ourselves helpless with various notions and pretenses. We must forget our personal goals and tasks, for every game has *its own subjective goal*, its own individual task. We must surrender ourselves to this goal—the more naively, spontaneously, and fully the better.

And when this joyful moment of life comes upon us we must treasure it, protect it, and love it, forgetting everything and living only in this moment as in a hidden, fleeting, but lovely little world…

All that remains then is to enjoy it gratefully, and in this enjoyment to find healing.

And if an unwonted moment comes upon us and our joy shatters "in a fine mist," we must never complain, lament, or, God forbid, despair. We must simply say "forgive me," gently and gratefully, to the vanished moment, and then gladly and calmly start from the beginning.

This is what I learned from the soap bubble. And if anyone thinks that my story is in itself no more than a soap bubble, let him try to gain from it the wisdom I received from this light, fleeting, but enchanting creation, and perhaps he will be successful…

Clouds

I fell in love with clouds as a child. I did not know why, and could not tell then what so captivated me, but I could admire them for hours on end. They seemed like living creatures that swam off into a blessed distance and called me to come with them; life was so airy, light, and joyful there. All sorts of welcome dreams awoke in my soul as wonderful fairy tales took shape in those clouds. I would gaze on those airy stories until my neck ached and my head began to gently spin. The adults would call me a daydreamer, and I would walk around for a time as one intoxicated. Oh, the beloved friends of my childhood reveries, so meek, gentle, and radiant! We never asked anything of each other, never promised each other anything; they simply floated above me and I admired them, and forgot my childish woes...

I have grown up long since, but the child still lives in me and rejoices in its old and eternally young friends. And yet they say that there are no lasting attachments on this earth! Whenever life becomes burdensome to me, when my life circumstances seem beyond my strength, I turn to the clouds; I embark on contemplation of them and find comfort therein.

Suddenly, completely unexpectedly, we find ourselves in an unknown world governed by other laws and happily inviting us into its makeup. How wonderfully the clouds rise up above everything, and how lightly; their weightlessness is effortless, intrinsic, and natural to them. That is why they are so light, so humble, so free of any pretenses; they are probably unaware of their own magnificence and grandeur... Or do they perhaps vaguely perceive that mighty, immeasurable, and divine height that stretches out above them?

And then that quiet, that calm, that wonderful stillness! It flows out of them and is perceived by us as a release, a pardon, a liberation. The Lermontovian desire to become like them is born in the depth of one's soul—to adopt their carefree nature, the serenity of their airy games, the painless and passive essence of these children of the light.

How quickly they come into being! How meekly they merge, dissipate, and melt away; how willingly they vanish without a trace, accepting their fate, giving in to the slightest breeze. And yet still at times we fancy that they are confidently and diligently floating towards their goal, as if they know exactly where they are hurrying.

Their image, shape, and makeup are eternally changing. Each moment renews them; every hour makes them unrecognizable; every day brings us something unprecedented and unique: an inexhaustible wealth of airy formations; unexpected combinations of existence and nonexistence, emptiness and plenty; unusual, indescribable shades of light and shadow, dull grey and exultant colors. One minute we see the simplicity of a milky covering and in the next the translucence of the finest netting, or a complex gathering of heavy masses. And sometimes their appearance strangely resembles our own earthly forms. Are those not mountains rising in the distance, cloaking the horizon? And there, the ruins of a heavenly castle? How mysterious is this mouth of a giant cave! Dragons creep by and disappear, reclining fir trees float past, the wings of angels form and are carried away. Weightless ringlets curl like whirlwinds, airy ships swim by, grim and playful visions arise. Then everything vanishes and suddenly there is not a cloud in the blue sky. So much wonderful poetry, so many blessed possibilities, so many momentary poems brought to life and reclaimed by an unknown poet of creation. Everything is always wonderful, wonderful and tremendous, even when it blends together into a grey, somber, hopeless shroud. It is a great sight, a generous gift, a heavenly painting, a conversation with God and a divine comfort.

This gift is given to deliver us from our tortured, overtaxed world with its malice and burdens, its unreasonable demands. A door is opened for us into a kingdom of gentle carelessness and wonderful indifference. Here nothing is required of us; we are neither threatened with anything nor forced to do something. We don't need to desire, acquire, judge, reject, concentrate, or remember. Here, we don't need to fight or resent. Here, we can forget. Let the overtaxed will slumber, let the intense thoughts disappear, let the grieving and wounded heart find peace. A person gives himself over to a relaxed and liberated perspective; he receives the joy of pure and selfless contemplation; he enters into a certain godly theater, ancient as the world, noble as its Creator.

The clouds give us forgetfulness of self; they lead us away from daily cares, ease and calm our anger, and still every spasm of our soul, quenching its greediness, dispelling its shadows, and softening its stubbornness—so serene and free is their flow, so meek and noble their lighthearted essence. The hardened will is pacified, and one begins to experience a sweet lack of desire and the right to a lack of will. The overtired mind is at rest: the absence of thoughts proves to be a source of intoxicating peace, a delightfully scattered and naïve absentmindedness. The ailing heart ceases to love, or not to love, to call out and be indignant, as the serenity of quiet, humility, and gratitude is poured into it like a balm. The entire soul is cleansed by contemplating this symbol of earthly detachment and heavenly grace—a generosity that heals and forgives all.

If we contemplated the clouds longer and more often, we would probably become better people. For they are living tales, stories that tell of the fulfillment of impossible dreams—or perhaps they are truly shades of the higher heavenly powers. Perhaps they are smoke from a censer, fanning billows around the invisible altar of God. Why does my heart tremble with anticipation when the setting sun illuminates a mighty, threatening cloud, as if blessing it and granting it unforeseen beauty? Why do I sometimes feel that the Almighty Lord Himself could tread on those clouds, in all their strength and glory? Is this perhaps a memory from beyond the reaches of time, awakening to the ancient way of things? Or was I perhaps a cloud once, now joyfully recognizing my ancient brothers?

He who contemplates clouds and lives in them with his heart sees dreams in his waking hours—dreams of a possible and approaching perfection. Perhaps these are dreams of the divine thoughts of God, departing from His bosom in light breaths...

About Deprivation

When I turned eight, my grandmother gave me a beautiful notebook bound in blue Morocco leather for Christmas, saying: "This is a journal for you to write about things that seems wise and good; let each of us write something in it as a keepsake." What a disappointment! How I wanted tin soldiers—I even dreamed of them at night. And suddenly, instead—a journal. How boring... But my grandfather took my journal and wrote on the first page: "If you want happiness, don't think of what you don't have; learn to go without unnecessary things." Yes, it was easy for him to say, "Don't think of it," when I was injured to the point of tears. But I had to accept it...

I didn't realize at the time how offended I was by this unpleasant life advice from my grandfather. At first I didn't even want to hear it; it was a direct mockery of me and my tin soldiers. But later, and after many years, I have had so many deprivations in life. And when I keenly lacked something, or when I was forced to part with something I loved, I always thought of the Morocco leather notebook and of grandfather's saying. Even now I call it "the rule of happiness," or "the law of the tin soldier." I think it also has something to do with Andersen's "The Brave Tin Soldier." The little one was brave—he went through fire and water without even blinking an eye...

And now this rule seems to me an expression of true wisdom to live by. Life is a battle that we must win; the victor is he who learns to personify goodness and justice. Of course all sorts of temptations and dangers arise, and each danger is in essence a threat. If we examine these threats, we understand that they are all virtually the same: *they are all threats of loss.* This is because so-called "humiliation" is also a loss of freedom, a loss of recognition by others, and a loss of financial success; these deprivations can of course be more difficult. We should never accept the loss of our own true dignity or our self-respect, but we should not take to heart the

absence of recognition by others, or denigration and slander. We must
know how to go without life "success," "esteem," or so-called "glory."

And so, if I should be afraid of these and similar deprivations,
I should have to deprive myself of the most important thing—
objective[8] *success in life*—as well as victory in the battle of life. And
if I desire an objective victory, I must *defy deprivation and despise
threats of loss.* What they call "iron-clad nerves" is nothing but a
courageous approach to impending or already occurring deprivation.
Everything that threatens me (and what is more, often only threatens
without ever being realized) is a form of deprivation—of food, drink,
clothing, warmth, comfort, possessions, health, etc. Thus a person
who has given himself a serious life task, who has great goals and
desires objective success and victory, must *not be afraid* of deprivation;
courage in the face of deprivation and the threat of loss is already
half the battle, like passing an "exam" for victory. He who trembles
over his comforts and enjoyments, his possessions and peace and
quiet, exposes his weakness to the enemy; he presents his Achilles'
heel and will soon be wounded in it; he will be disadvantaged,
powerless, bound, and enslaved. He can expect to fail in life…

We are threatened with deprivation our entire lives. Our
lives are plagued with thoughts and worries over these possible losses,
casualties, humiliation, and poverty. But this is what constitutes the
school of life; in this lies our preparation for success and training
for victory. This school requires us to *spiritually defeat* threats and
deprivation. The ability to lightly bear our cares, to easily forego
that which we lack, constitutes the art of living. No loss or privation
should disturb our soul's equilibrium: "There isn't enough? Let it be.
I will make do."

We should never forfeit the blessed and significant things in
life; we should never refuse the most important thing for which we
wage battle. However, those things that are insignificant and

---

[8] *Translator's note:* The Russian word "predmet" is translatable as both "object" and "subject,"
and consequently "predmetno" can mean both "objective" and "subjective". It has been the
translator's choice to translate "predmet" as "object" in the context of the author's philosophy
unless it is clear that he means "subject."

menial—the trivialities of life—should neither blind nor bind us,
nor render us helpless, nor enslave us.

The art of overcoming deprivation is achieved on two
conditions.

Firstly, a person must have in life a certain *higher, discerning
value* that he truly loves above all things, and which truly *deserves*
his love. This value is what keeps him alive, and for which he fights;
it illuminates his life and directs his creative power; in its presence
everything else pales and retreats into the background. This is the
holy and sanctifying *sun of love*, in the light of which no deprivation
seems difficult, or threat terrifying. Such is the path of every hero, of
all the faithful, every confessor and martyr…

Secondly, a person must have the ability to *concentrate* his
attention, love, will, and imagination—not on what he lacks, that of
which he is deprived—but on *what he is given.* He who constantly
thinks of what he is missing will always be hungry, envious, and laden
with hatred. Forever thinking about privations can drive a person
insane, or lay him in his grave; trembling constantly over potential
losses demeans him and leads to enslavement. On the other hand,
he who grows accustomed to and recognizes with love what is given
him will find in every triviality *a new depth and beauty* for his life, as
if it were a *doorway to spiritual expanses*, an entryway to God's hidden
garden, a well generously pouring forth spring water from its living
depths. For such a person, a simple flower is enough to bring him
into contact with God's creation and cause him to bow down before
it in amazement. For him, as for Spinoza, simply watching a spider
is enough to comprehend the law and order of nature; like Diogenes,
he needs only a simple ray of sunshine in order to encounter the nature
of self-evidence and lose himself in its experience. The disciples of
Anthony the Great once asked him how he could see the Lord God.
He answered them in the following manner: "In the early morning,
when I come out of my mud hut into the desert, I see the sun rise, I
hear the birds sing, a quiet breeze blows on my face—and my heart
sees the Lord and sings for joy."

The poor man possesses such wealth, if he knows how to be rich…

This also means that deprivation urges us towards a dedicated contemplation of the world, as if a certain mystical voice were saying to us: "What you have already been given conceals *true wealth*; feel it, master it, and forego everything else that you were not given, for you do not need it…" In all earthly things there is a *measurement of depth*. In this depth is hidden the door to wisdom and blessedness. How often "wealth" disguises sheer paucity and pitiful squalor, while poverty can prove to be veritable wealth if a person has spiritually overcome his impoverished state…

For this reason it is not good for a person to forego deprivations. They are necessary for him and can bring him true wealth, which he would not otherwise achieve. Deprivation forges a person's character; it fosters victory in him as in Suvorov; it teaches him internal contemplation and promises to reveal to him the path to wisdom.

I do not bewail the deprivations and loss that have visited me in life. Rather, I often look back with gratitude on the blue Morocco leather notebook that once taught me "the law of the tin soldier." At the time it cost me a desired toy, but it revealed to me the way to true wealth. I would not like to be deprived of *that* in my life…

About Health

How tedious to always be thinking about one's health—to take eternal precautions, fear everything, do without every forbidden thing and always ask, "Will this or that harm me?" One's entire life becomes full of fear and dread. You watch your every step, live under scrutiny, and become your own prison guard. The joy goes out of life. Suspicion and hypochondria take over one's soul. It is not a life, but a wretched existence. Who would need such a life and why?

In this way I complained to my grandfather in a letter, when my lungs were beginning to develop something and I had to lie in a sanatorium for many months. How depressing it was! Nothing but the thermometer (which I used to call a "prisonmeter"[9]) three times a day... I was young, agile, talkative, and had just begun an interesting research project that required constant library research and the copying of texts. Furthermore, I was in love, and unsure of her feelings for me. Oh, how anxious I was then!

My dear grandfather...although he passed away long ago, I kept the letter he sent me in reply. It is so significant, so thoughtfully profound, that it must without doubt be published. My grandfather's philosophy grew from the heart; it was nourished by contemplation and incorporated into his life. However, no great philosophical works survived him.

Here is his letter, word for word.

"Oh, my impatient one," he wrote, "why are you so anxious? I can see by your letter that you are suffering. Please calm yourself and don't make it difficult for your Doctor. No, I don't mean your sanatorium doctor, God bless him; he will do his job no matter what. I mean, of course, *your inner Doctor*, with whom you are at odds. Do you not know anything about him? Then let me tell you. Lie back a bit more comfortably, if you please. Just like that, on your back... Comfortable? Well, now, don't be so tense, and don't have such a somber expression on your face! If you give in to dismal thoughts, then you will neither hear me nor understand anything of my story. Please don't furrow your brow. Breathe calmly and deeply, as if you wanted to go to sleep. There, now listen to me with your heart and examine within yourself every word I write.

"Every one of us has our own inner Doctor. We cannot see or hear him. He leads a hidden, mysterious life, never answering questions directly. But we can and must hearken to him. From time to time we see him in our dreams, but we don't usually know it is he. In those instances we dream about a nice, amiable person, in whom we have complete trust: he is very sympathetic, accompanying us,

---

[9] *Translator's note:* In the original Russian, the words "thermo" and "prison" sound very similar, so the play on words is much more effective.

silently helping us in various matters, and leading us away from trouble. Usually we do not even see his face; he seems to live in shadows, and yet we feel his kind, caring nature; we awaken with a feeling of gratitude, encouraged and comforted... This is our inner Doctor, who is given to us for the duration of our lives and with whom we must exist in harmony.

"You will ask, of course, how you can reach him. Do you not see? We have a unique gift of heeding our inner contemplation, and we must put it to good use. We must heed the existence of our own instinct—that great and wise subconscious power without which our life would be completely impossible. This power develops and builds the human makeup—the amazing coexistence, the earthly cohabitation of our bodies and souls. It cares about us, guides and protects us, lives in every element of our being. You can say that God gives every person a certain inner 'builder.' He awakens you in the morning because you have slept enough; indeed, *he* is the one who "awakens" you from the inside, when other people can only "wake you up." You have probably seen people whom it is impossible to fully rouse. It is clear why: you may forcefully and arbitrarily wake them up, but they are organically-internally asleep...

"You may slip while walking—but *he* has already taken care that you do not fall: he has supported your balance. You cut your finger, but everything is already arranged so that all your blood doesn't flow out, and while your wound heals it is internally tended by your caring Doctor. Whatever you may take on, he looks after you constantly. You worked hard today, but would still like to stay up over your books the entire night. He considers this harmful and announces it to you through fatigue and drowsiness. And if you insist on your own way by starting to smoke a lot, or drinking strong coffee, you will end up at odds with him and he may announce an internal "strike." A difficult and demanding day has passed; it is time for you to sleep, and he signals this to you: your eyes close of their own accord, you start to yawn and become lethargic and sleepy. From him come feelings of hunger, thirst, cold, boredom, and depression. You fail to take care of yourself, you don't know what you need, while he knows every requirement of your bodily system and takes care of you. It is he who warns you that you need more carbohydrates (sugars), less salt, a lot more vitamins. Goosebumps come from him, as well as sneezes, toothaches, fevers, and coated tongues.[10] If you do not consider these things, so much the worse for you; he can't and won't persuade you, but he will make you weak and sick... Come to your senses and change your mind; if you find yourself cornered, at a dead end, look for a way out...

"He always notifies you about overindulgence (wine) or negligence (a frozen nose). A living person is a whole system of balances: a balance of warmth, food, sleep-and-wakefulness; a balance in the pressure of muscles and nerves and blood circulation; moderation in movement and rest, moderation in sadness and joy, moderation in sensual pleasures and chastity, moderation in concentration of thought, moderation in distractions and entertainment. It is he who supervises the necessary amounts and proper balances: he knows what you need, he limits your ability to work, he sends you a migraine, insomnia, or the desire to jump and run; he lays you down into a warm bed, or arranges for you a long-lasting neurosis.

"He encourages the pregnant woman to eat chalk and charcoal because they are essential for the child. When you approach an invisible danger in the dark, he warns you with a beating heart and a feeling of unexplained dread. You must train yourself to heed all these things. The mysterious Doctor of your instinct is wiser and more farsighted than you. He requires balance, expediency, and moderation in all things. He is the embodiment of silent, creative wisdom. From us he requires *attention and obedience*, in exchange for which he gives us health: a self-sustaining balance in life, a light, vigorous state of being...

---

[10] *Translator's note:* In the Russian folk medicine tradition, a tongue with a white coating was considered a symptom of a coming or present illness.

"The ability to heed the wordless voice of one's inner Doctor has, unfortunately, been lost by modern man. The original man had this gift and was happy. But today's unfortunate pundit is not capable of this. He prides himself on his rational thinking and imagines that conscious thought composes the main essence and force of life. He imagines that culture has overcome and subjugated nature. He is a proud, self-righteous rationalist who thinks his arbitrary rule is designed to conquer God-created nature, or perhaps even take its place. He goes as far as to think up various unnatural theories and ways of life, turning everything upside down. His godlessness blinds him more and more, luring him farther and farther away. The sin of *going against nature* is imbedded deeper and deeper in modern man—and it is too late for him to escape fair retribution. A person's stubborn defiance of nature can break his back, for he who rises against God-created nature *rebels against God*.

"This is why we must turn back to *God-created nature* in order to receive heaven's gifts again. We must learn to live in harmony with our instinctive builder and mysterious Doctor. We must learn to inquire from him without hoping for a verbal answer. What would he like, what would he wish us to avoid, what suits him—and what does he decidedly reject as something harmful? It is no use to try to outwit him, or to be contriving. Consulting with your Doctor does not mean indulging your passions and wishes. It is something completely different. A person focuses on his internal self and listens to the voice of his bodily system; he heeds the voice of his instinct, but not his blind and passionate side—not his spirit-contradicting greed, but his *spiritual wisdom*, given to him by God and nourished by nature. It is as if a person resurrects in himself the act through which *the spirit governs instinct to its very depths and from its very depths*. He consults with the *spirit of his instinct* and embodies it in the image of his 'Doctor.' This awakens in the soul an ancient, primeval depth that perhaps had completely withered away, or perhaps was only depleted by rational thought. The person knocks at the door of his God-given and natural Doctor, desiring to partake of his homespun wisdom and restore in himself the organic experience of nature. The Doctor answers without words: his wisdom is not logical, but organic; he silently prescribes what is needed; he affirms, confirms, or rejects, but does not advise. There, in the very depths of our instinctive spirituality, lives a fertile seed of health, that wonderful gift of *organic self-healing* with which we must enter into communion.

"This is the heart of the matter, my impatient boy! You have wasted that immediate, living connection with your builder and Doctor; as a result, you became ill. Now you must at all costs restore that connection. You must not only recover from your cough and heal your 'injured' lung; you must begin a new way of life. You must enter into the organic rhythm of nature, as if you were plunging into a stream of self-healing and natural self-sustainment. This can't be done by force, by simple decision, or on short notice. You must gradually become used to the thought that here you must obey, not command; instead of exploiting your strength at will, you must preserve moderation of effort and balance in your entire life. Only by *submitting to nature* can we govern over it. He who lives and creates together with nature, out of nature, is embraced willingly and joyfully by nature. For nature, akin to fate, leads the obedient man and forcefully drags the insubordinate man. For this reason, if you will trust your instinctual Doctor and listen to his quiet instructions and warnings, you will not have to worry constantly about your health: he will do that for you. You will live, love, and create, and he will support your wellbeing. You will observe his organic wishes, and he will welcome all your spiritual needs. Together you will be a living, healthy whole. You will be in good health and will enjoy a wonderful, confident peace of mind with regard to yourself and your affairs.

"There it is, my dear. Health is something bigger than people usually think. Good health is a divinely prescribed and God-pleasing harmony between a person's own nature and spirit. Every person is created for good health and designed to be healthy.

In an ailing state, we correspond neither to our calling nor to God's design; what pleasure can our disfigurement and torment bring Him? He sends us ailments so that we can recover from them, like a path towards wellbeing. Thus, sickness is like a mysterious notation we must decipher: it describes our former, incorrect life, and then the new, wise, and healthy life that awaits us. We must decipher this 'code,' interpret it, and put it to use. That is the point of sickness.

"All of this is a miracle—a living miracle of nature, a great miracle of God, one that we usually don't notice. We pass it by, and our deadened hearts remain cold and indifferent. Just think how wonderful it is: in each of us lies the ability to realize within ourselves a divinely conceived harmony of spirit, soul, and body; each of us is given the gift of a hidden builder and Doctor, who is designed to implement this harmony. Each of us has the gift of retreating into our own spirit and invoking this prescribed and promised harmony—in other words, of immediately *returning to nature and submitting ourselves to the will of God...*

"But you must not take me at my word. Try to see all of this with your own eyes. Take advantage of your illness for this purpose: it should not only heal you (for that is the point of its existence) but also enlighten you. Wisdom is attained only through trials and suffering. So you must not be angry at your illness; rather, give yourself some rest, imagine that you have embarked on some travels and must bring with you your friendship with your Doctor, the gift of health, and organic wisdom. Having experienced this by yourself, you must test it, make certain of it until it becomes self-evident. For this you will need patience. Everything that is wonderful on earth grows and develops slowly. And you specifically need what is wonderful—a divinely prescribed worldwide harmony. Plant it within yourself, and then every aspect of your life—love, family, creativity, old age—will be illumined in a new way..."

Since then I have indeed experienced all of this; I have tested it, made certain of it, until it became self-evident. As for grandfather's letter, I have read and re-read it many times, and now I know it almost completely by heart...

The World's Dust

It lies hidden, a soft layer in the furrows of a village road, awaiting any excuse to soar up in flight, whether from playing a game with the wind, or from a horse stirring it up with its hoof or the wheel of a wagon. Any reason will do. It flies up and clings to the traveler, and he will not easily be rid of it. And if a real windstorm were to come and begin to blow, it will fly up in a spiral, soaring and exulting... Dust is everywhere you look. Millions of weightless specks of dust fly golden in a sunbeam: they sparkle colorfully, then disappear into the shadows, and thus the shadows are full of them too... If you are hammering or sweeping, it flies around freely: if you blow it aside, heavy grains of dust quietly settle into bags and bins. In vain do housewives try to remove it by beating it out of carpets and washing it off furniture: they merely rouse it from sleep and fill the air with it. Dust settles onto the black faces of chimney sweeps and coalminers; it is caked in layers on forgotten books; it forever seeks a hiding place in the world's expanses. And when a sandstorm lifts the sands of the desert and carries them like a tornado towards a traveler, it eclipses the very sun and breathes destruction onto his head.

If you think about it and look around, you will find dust everywhere: in the ashes of the fireplace; on the fresh apple; in people's lungs as well as in their chatter; in the lonely soul and the foolish book; in the tail of a comet and in the disintegration of society; and especially in every civil war and revolution. The winds of life circle it into all the empty spaces: prodigal, uprooted, adrift; harmless at first glance, in fact it is burdensome, unhappy, abandoned, and unsettled. For it fell away from the order of the world, could not find its place in the sound harmony of life, and became a living symbol of worldwide chaos and the world's downfall. Dust is a turbulent multitude: it is the chaos of the world's unemployed, it is impending dissolution and decay.

The world longs for unity and organization: its life is spent fighting for a constructive, living order. The purpose of the world's diversity is to achieve true coexistence, noble service, and balance through creation. It is the same in every stage of life: in the human cell and in the great orbit of the planets, in the dust of the field and in a person's soul, in the creation of art and in the society of men. Everywhere the world lives according to its *needs*, eliminating the *unnecessary*. And in that place where the unnecessary things have been banished, they either disintegrate into ashes of earth or come together to form a new and sickly being, foreboding destruction and decay.

And so in the great productive cycle of the world even a small atom has a purpose: it must comprehend its true nature and its relationship to the whole, establish its free will and existence, and willingly be integrated into the general fabric of the universe, into its working order. If the atom succeeds in doing this, it will lead a good and happy life; it will grow and bear fruit, and its fruit will be its service to the greater work of the world. But if it is unsuccessful, it will discover neither its service nor its rank; it will find itself fallen away and rootless, lonely and unsettled. It then becomes the world's dust. The lonely and unemployed particle of dust, aimlessly wandering through life, is tossed about from place to place like a rejected outcast, an aimless idler, an orphaned child of the world. Its life is deprived of meaning and purpose, for it has neither a nourishing foundation nor an organic sense of coexistence; all it can do is wander aimlessly about, languishing away or lashing out in rebellion... Something that has broken away from the world is not part of the universal choir, and its individual voice does not create its own unique and faithful melody. It doesn't share in the burden of the world's existence, and for this reason its own burden in life becomes unbearable. The joys of reconciliation, inclusion, and universal brotherhood are not bestowed upon it. It has another fate: that of eternal homelessness, eternal grievance, and eternal protest, until it finally discovers its calling, find its natural place—its *service*, and thus its *happiness*, for there is no happiness on earth without service, or peace in isolation. An atom of the world that has found itself *in the world* is no longer a victim of circumstance nor a child of chaos: it secures its *freedom* in serving the *needs of the world*. It becomes part of the universal choir, singing praises...

It is true that a certain worldly wisdom dictates that even dust may be used as a passive instrument, that it is a blind as well as a suffering agent: perhaps disconnected and miserable, but still useful to the whole; perhaps discordant and rebellious, but still compelled to obey, so that even chaos serves a purpose in the universe, in some mysterious way. But this pitiless wisdom gives the disconnected atom neither gratification nor peace, but rather leaves it to suffer blindly and curse its fate. A child who is cast out by the world, who is ever swept away and thrown out, wandering the far reaches of the world like the Wandering Jew, can find no comfort in the thought that even dust, and dirt, and bacteria, and evil people play some sort of undefined role in the grand "scheme of things." This thought gives him neither deliverance nor happiness. All the unsettled atoms of the world form one great universal problem, a great disaster, an impending danger. Sooner or later they begin to unite in opposition, whether in the cosmic expanse or the sand-swept desert, or in the form of a sickly newfangled organism, or in the shape of a social revolution or civil war... This is the great "organizational" purpose of the world: dust must be accepted and included in the living order of the world and society; dust must receive deliverance from us as well as healing and happiness through willing service. This purpose cannot be achieved in a minute, nor in an hour; this is no random ailment that can be healed with a single prescription. No, this purpose is for all of time: it is eternal, demanding both constant effort and the simultaneous development of wise and careful means. For the great cycle and formation of the world will repeatedly see newly appearing atoms that have fallen away and been discarded, that are unsettled and have "lost their head," unable to fold themselves into the work of the whole. And there will always be a possibility that such wandering atoms, rebellious and callous, will flock together and break into a dark hymn of malice and rejection, protesting against the Creator who found no place for them, bringing jealousy and hatred into the universe, bearing revenge and enslavement to other people and forcing equalization upon them...

However, the great problem of dust has yet another side, another meaning. A person's internal life contains its own disintegration, its unique dust. Living from day to day, we fail to notice when our soul becomes covered with the dust of insignificant daily trifles and begins to grow shallow, to dissipate and deteriorate as a result. Every human soul is designed to become part of a harmonious whole, living and acting out of one spiritual center. A person's character must be firmly rooted in the spirit. He must be like a city with a single impenetrable fortress housing the city's sacred relics. Or he must be like the creative process behind a work of art that is founded on one main idea. For this reason he cannot allow his life to be swallowed up in dust or to disintegrate into meaningless trifles.

This is why we must constantly distinguish between things essential to the spirit and things that are meaningless, to distinguish the primary from the secondary, the principal from the trivial, the sacred and significant from the insignificant and vacuous. We must do all this in order to place a steady, rhythmic accent on the things that are purposeful and sacred in our lives. This does not mean that we avoid all trivialities and become self-important, pedantic, or sanctimonious; rather, it means that we must strengthen our spiritual sense and become discerning. We must ensure that the things which make up our lives are in contact with our spiritual center. We must measure them against our spirit's light and substance, so that they shine forth from within it and thus reveal their true meaning. If they can withstand the light of this central fire and are proven to be justified, they are good things; they are deemed worthy of being chosen and preferred, while the things that cannot be justified in our lives will naturally be exposed and fall away. This is the process of purification from our soul's dust. Not everything is good for our spiritual organism and its internal makeup. That which cannot be of service to it must break away and live outside our internal space. To live means to discern, to evaluate and choose; if we never learn how to do this, we will be inundated by the dust of life. To live means building a foundation on essential things, and to shape from them our character and our life views. If we are not capable of this, we will disintegrate into dust and lose our very selves…

Every insignificant triviality of our existence—every misfortune; every base and empty circumstance of life which attains weight and "significance" in our eyes, but which is really devoid of higher purpose; every vacuous and vagabond factor of life that assails us without interruption, every numbing banality that claims our time and attention, irritating, agitating, and disappointing us, distracting, exhausting, and draining us—all these things are *dust*, that same ill-fated and pitiful dust of life… And if we cannot be rid of it but rather live with it instead, giving away to it the fire of our existence, never developing within ourselves a finer sense of taste, never counteracting it with a stronger and nobler depth of spirit, then its vulgarity will devour us. Our life's actions will squander our higher purpose; they will become meaningless and irresponsible. Our quality of life will become base; our love will become capricious, impure, and fruitless; our actions will become random, faithless, and treacherous; our spirit will be stifled by the dust of life…

Then our life will truly become "a vain gift, a chance gift;"[11] it will have squandered its purpose and spiritual definition. A person who has reached this point wanders as if in a fog and sees, in Plato's words, only the empty shadows of existence.[12] Brought in by the dust, he himself stirs up clouds of dust—and for that reason he does not see the sun for the dust he has raised, in the words of Bishop

---

[11] A.S. Pushkin.
[12] Plato. *Republic*.

Berkeley.[13] And when he is seized by passions, the very dampness of these passions, when mixed with the dust of his vacuous life, becomes a sticky mud in which he rejoices, as Heraclitus wrote...[14]

Hidden beside the pathways of our life, this cunning dust lies all around us; it is better for us not to disturb it, nor send it wafting in the wind. It steals unnoticed into the inner chamber of our soul and settles on everything that lies hidden there. This is why we must be able clean it from our internal space—and if we do not develop this skill, we risk being suffocated by our own dust. For dust causes everything inside a person to decay: his thoughts, theoretically "combining" relative abstract concepts (logical dust); his ungrounded imagination, subjectively toying with images (aesthetic dust); his will, disconnected from its sacred roots, cynical, power-hungry, and cruel (political dust); and his cold and deadened heart, which has forgotten how to love and is covered with the morally indifferent dust of life.

If the heart has grown cold, then the person is half-dead; he will not be able to challenge the dust. And so the crisis of the modern world is the crisis of the deadened heart and the rising of the dust.

About Generosity

You never knew my great-grandfather? What a pity! He was a kind and charming man. He was seventy-six years old when the Lord took him away to His dwelling. He was a woodcarver, a great master. The delicate work came remarkably easily to him: it was like lace, truly, and done with such taste! He was happiest when he could give the

---

[13] *Translator's note:* George Berkeley. "We have first raised a dust and then complain we cannot see."
[14] *Translator's note:* Heraclitus. "They vainly purify themselves by defiling themselves with blood, just as if one who had stepped into the mud were to wash his feet in mud. And they pray to these images, as if one were to talk with a man's house, knowing not what gods or heroes are."

finest little piece to someone important and talented. Smiling his happy smile, he would say on such occasions: "It was a way for me to enter into his life, to help him find in life at least some small joy."

Oh, so you did meet him? ...Yes, yes, that was he, with long white hair, a high forehead, eyes somewhat absent and full of dreams, and an unforgettable smile: it was as if everything around him was smiling... Yes, and during his last years he walked hunched over a little. I wanted to tell you a little bit about him.

You see, when I observe modern life, it often seems to me that people lend excessive value to material belongings or riches, as if considerable means were equivalent to considerable happiness. This is entirely untrue. Whoever thinks and feels that way will probably lead an unhappy life. This is what I learned from my late great-grandfather.

For his entire life he was compelled to earn his bread, and this was not always easy; and yet in spite of this he was one of the happiest people in the world. You may ask how this was possible. It was because of what he called "the art of ownership"—in other words, generosity.

He was the seventh in his family, and the youngest: all were boys. The elder brothers were callous and greedy. They looked down on him with contempt and never gave him anything. His parents died early, and he was barely able to finish the local school. When he did, his brothers announced to him: "Go ahead and earn your own bread." He didn't like arguments or disputes, so he began to study what really interested him: woodcarving and violin playing. The woodcarving came to him naturally; his work was well liked. He explained it in the following way: "I do this *from the soul*, with love, and people feel that; they go through life searching for love, they hunger for it; that is why they like my work."

A year later he was not only earning his own bread (life was inexpensive then), but also paying for violin lessons. Then he left his brothers and began to live with his childless uncle. His aunt loved

him very much; she called him "my little dove." And it was true:
he did have something dove-like about him. As for his incomplete
education, he later built upon it with insatiable reading.

Sometimes he simply took the violin bow into his hands,
and the melody would start to flow. Everyone would sit and listen,
enchanted, their eyes full of tears. You would forget your life's grief:
it was as if all your cares and burdens were lifted from your shoulders
and your heart was singing. How he played Russian folk songs, and
what's more, in their ancient folkloric arrangements and harmonies!
He later kept company with Melgunov and was great friends with
gusli[15] players. Sometimes he would appear serious and reverent, but
his eyes would shine with bliss.

You ask about "the art of ownership"? Just a moment, just
a moment, I will tell you… He did not know poverty, but neither
was he ever wealthy. Twice he was matched with wealthy brides. He
told me about it himself: "They were both made of hard wood and
crudely fashioned. You can't love such women. There was no song in
them. And they didn't understand anything about ownership: they
adored their wealth—you could see it in their faces. With every one
of us, *the most important thing* shows in our eyes—and in their eyes
was greed." Later, he married my great-grandmother and lived with
her, two souls as one. She was unusually kind, poor but intelligent,
and the leading singer at weddings; she knew all the old wedding
songs, and people would listen to her with bated breath as soon as
she broke out in song.

When my great-grandfather began, as it happened, to tell
stories or give counsel, I could listen to him for hours on end. Later,
I even began to write things down for memory's sake. Here is what I
wrote down about ownership.

"Listen, child," he said to me once, "owning things is a
special art; and this art is the secret to life happiness. The main thing
here is *not to depend on your possessions*, not to swear by them.

---

[15] *Translator's note:* A Russian multi-stringed instrument, similar to a dulcimer or lyre.

Our possessions should serve us and submit to us. That way they never dare to strive higher and thus rule over us. It's either one or the other—either you control them, or they will walk all over you. Moreover, possessions are sly-y-y. As soon as they notice that you are subservient to them, they will immediately oppress and exhaust you. Then just wait; they will engulf your spirit and body completely. That is the end: your possessions will take your place and become your master, and you will be their slave. They will become the most important thing in your life, and you will be their accessory. But the most important thing is this: man must be free, not only from the oppression of people, but also from the *oppression of his possessions.* What kind of freedom is it, if you are independent of people but enslaved to your possessions? A free man must be free in regards to his wealth. I have control, and my possessions submit to me. Then I am truly *in power,* for the power is in my hands. You cannot quake and tremble over your wealth. Whoever is afraid *for* his wealth trembles *before* it: he does so lest it leave him and plunge him into poverty. Such a person's possessions, like a vampire in the night, begin to prey upon him and demean him, though some day, if only at the hour of his death, they will abandon him once and for all...

"So here, as you see, I am carving wood. I am able to do this because I use my carving knife and can do whatever I want with the wood. This is how I am able to put my whole heart into my carving and show people what kind of gentle beauty and joy can exist in this world.

"Or here—the violin. The bow and the strings should listen to me; they should sing in the same way my soul sings. Love is *my* master, and I am the *violin's* master; thus it in turn sings to you every joy of life, and of God's beauty.

"It is the same with possessions. They are not given to us to absorb our love, nor exhaust our hearts. On the contrary, they are designed to *serve our heart and express our love.* Otherwise possessions become a burden, an idol, a penal servitude. Not in vain does the Gospel speak of Mammon. He who believes in God cannot believe in wealth. He who bows before his own or another man's wealth, even once, will not even notice when he begins to serve the devil...

"The answer does not lie in putting away or forbidding all possessions; this would be foolish, unnatural, and harmful. Rather we should *take control* of our possessions instead of eliminating them, and thus become *free of them*. This freedom cannot come from other people; we must claim it ourselves, we must free our souls. If it is easy for me to think about my possessions, then I am free. I determine the fate of every one of my belongings, and I do this easily: my belongings obey me. My worth is not determined by my possessions; my fate does not depend on what I own; I am neither a dog chained to my possessions nor a guard watching over them by night; I am not a beggar asking a penny of every life occasion and hiding it away in a stocking. It is shameful to tremble over your belongings, and even more shameful to envy those who are wealthier than you. We must live in another manner entirely: we must easily withdraw from our bank account wherever there is a need, and give with joy wherever the heart moves us to do so, providing to him who is lacking, happily sacrificing without regrets, expecting nothing in return from him who is unable to give, and in a brotherly manner forgetting about collecting interest. Most importantly—listen, child—never tremble over your possessions: "The Lord gave, and the Lord hath taken away; blessed be the name of the Lord" (Job 1:21). He who trembles over his wealth demeans himself and loses his dignity, and it is better for a lowly person with lowly thoughts not to have any wealth at all..."

"It is written in wise books," he said to me once, "that possessions are an accumulated labor, but I think that both labor and possessions are *from* the spirit and *for* the spirit. And the spirit is first and foremost *love*. Thus, for the true human being, possessions are *provisions for the heart and instruments of love*. The rich man needs a generous heart; only then it can be considered that he has earned his wealth. A lot of money and a limited heart means a difficult fate and a cruel demise."

Sometimes he would talk a little like this and then, taking up his violin, he would begin to play old Russian songs, one after another: "Our Faithful Well," "Do Not Sing, O Nightingale," and many more. I would sit and listen happily...

He carved all these things into my soul, and even now I can't listen to these songs with indifference. Oh, there is so much freedom and kindness in the Russian people! So much generosity, depth, and sincerity in their songs!

It seems to me that my great-grandfather thought and lived with true wisdom...

In the Early Morning

Why did I wake up so early today? Was it perhaps a moth thrashing about at sunrise? Or did the quiet rumblings of a distant thunder-storm reach me? Or did my soul feel that touch of silent reproach from an awakening world, the one which visits those who are submerged in their lonely dreams at dawn? I don't know. I only know that I jumped out of bed with the feeling that I would miss something important if I overslept; sleepy and confused, I opened the window onto the garden. And immediately I was swept away by a waft of young air, a gentle chill, the ravishing generosity of the world...

It wasn't yet quite dawn, but the night was already coming to an end. High, high in the pale sky, the stars were being quietly extinguished. The uncertain feeble light spilled forth from the east, as if timidly asking if it were time yet. ... The night shadows were melting away, yet still trying to preserve their secrets. With each passing minute, everything changed.

It was very humid all day yesterday; everything was stifled and made wretched by the heat. The earth swallowed so much of the sun's heat that it overflowed with it, and we, the pitiful people, lounged about languidly, exhaustedly, seeking some cool respite. Even the wind, with its hot, ailing breath, gave us no relief... Where was all this now? Where did it disappear? The air is pure and light; it blows cheerfully, playfully. It has recovered, reclaimed its freshness, and is intoxicated with a joy that quickly envelopes you, wakes you, and intoxicates you with bright anticipation. All of God's creation is swimming in this air, rejoicing in it, and answering with fragrances and songs.

The lilac smells sweetly, exhausted from its own generosity; a faint trace of the first lilies-of-the-valley is carried forth; the sour cherry tree pours out heavy waves of scent; and from time to time the breath of the pine tree fills the air.

And the birds are exultant; they whistle out everything at once, with such wholehearted sincerity that it seems as if they had their fill of silence during the night and are now bursting with news of their discoveries to the world; it is as if they have clearly and decidedly answered all of the world's questions and must now proclaim their decisions. Somewhere in the distance a nightingale is still twittering, but weakly and wearily now. In its place the other members of the bird population surrender themselves to whole-hearted rejoicing. All the air is filled with gentle warbling, cheerful chirping, nearby whistling, and faraway cawing; chatter, babbling, exclamations, and a loud, unexpected peep; brief pecking, extended calls, impatient trills, and an irritating rattle; interruptions, back-and-forth calls, sudden stops and bursts. It is a festive celebration for the birds, an avian madhouse. From the tall chestnut tree, an oriole drowns the others out with its authoritative announcements. All of these sounds are as brisk as the air itself. And the air gets lighter and lighter, as if giving way to the awakening colors of the world, while only the people continue to sleep through their depressing or provocative dreams...

Suddenly, a light—but wholly unique, a cool sigh, the trembling and rustling in the heights of a large poplar, a sliding whisper in the tall grass—and in the gently deepening blue of the sky a little sleepy cloud of light forms. A new day begins...

Why is this early morning hour so delightful? Where does its joy come from, filling the soul? What do we see, what do we perceive in these virginal moments of life? An ancient woman with shining eyes once told me about this, when I was still a child, and I believed her for the rest of my life.

"God's day, you see," she said, "is very light and gentle. It illuminates everything. It sees all, it hears and knows everything. And this is such a difficult thing... There is so much that is bad on earth, so much malice and sin! Can anyone bear such a thing? That is why the day cannot last long. It must hide away and retire; it must come to an end. It takes away with it every injury, every grief, all of the pain of mankind. And in its place comes the darkness of night, It scatters everyone, puts out every fire, stops every sin of the day so that nothing more can be seen and everything ceases to be. In the meantime, the day rests and recovers. And when the night comes on, the stars of God are lit; they shine meekly, pouring forth purity, giving peace to the world and grace to mankind. Through this purity and kindness of the stars, everything is cleansed; man's noise is calmed, the dust of the world settles, all poison of the spirit is dissolved, all heat of sin vanishes. The earth's air once again becomes light and immaculate. And God's day can begin once more..."

How she found all this out I do not know. It must be that she spent the day in torment, and then listened carefully all night long. But I believed her for the rest of my life. And when that happy hour comes nigh and I am able to see God's morning once again, in all its beauty and purity, I am firmly convinced that she had told me a truth about the world.

It is indeed true that our daily human actions raise a veritable cloud of earthly dust. It is indeed true that our wicked human passions defile and infect the earth's atmosphere. And it is also true that in the dusty, infected air of the earth it is impossible to lead a wonderful life, impossible to rejoice in the world's beauty or God's perfection. And if a grace-filled healing is not given us from above, does not cleanse us from our iniquity, where else can we hope for salvation?

And isn't it true that our daily life brings everything to light, baring before us all our wickedness, our cruelty, and the lowliness of the world, inflicting upon us one wound after another? Oh, how impressionable is the day! Oh, how fragile our childish perceptions! Oh, this sorrow for the aggrieved, and shame for the shameless! Sometimes, after only half the day, so much has already accumulated that it is impossible to breathe because of all the poisonous dust, and the light fades from our eyes. Then we must immediately cut short the day's stream of consciousness and seek healing in solitude. That is why the most sensitive and gentle people find relief from the day in even the briefest sleep...

The day holds worries and needs, while night is wealthy and free from cares. The day is restriction and tension, while night is freedom and limitlessness. The day is distress and exhaustion, while night is oblivion and forgetfulness. The day is a struggle; the night is peace. The day is labor, while night is a cherished dream. The day is presence, while night is rest and absence. The day is interaction, while night is disassociation and the quiet of solitude. And what would remain of us, born of this earth, if night did not give us respite, shelter, and forgiveness? Meanwhile, we cannot part with temptations and difficulties even in our sleep... What would become of us without this quiet oblivion, this healing darkness, this serene depth into which we quietly submerge ourselves in order to become one with blessed rest and limitless nightly visions?

The things of the earth quickly become tired: nature tires of its daily exertion; the day tires of our dust and our poison; we ourselves tire of our helplessness and ineptitude, our faithless dealings with others—our unloving, unfruitful, greedy, and wary response to people. And if healing and strength were not given us from above, where else could we expect salvation?

This is why help comes down to us from above. The light of day dies away. Dusk falls. Darkness grows. Faded colors die out.

Weary images lose their shape. Things that are light seem massive; heavy things become nearly weightless. At the very least a quiet darkness covers the indiscernible, vanishing expanse. The hour of parting draws nigh: all things bid each other farewell in order to rest from each other, withdraw into themselves, lose themselves in blessed solitude and enter into oblivion, a mysterious communion with the dormant world. Thus, all things secure their rest and purification.

Then the stars of God light up and bestow their rays upon the dusty and tired earth. Quietly, they pour forth their wisdom onto the earth, onto all of nature and mankind, onto every fatigued, dusty, and tainted thing. They send them purification and healing, so that they might imitate the stars; so that people might find quiet and peace among one another, for noise and anger are not from God; so that they might become meek and gentle, for crudeness and cruelty are a result of mankind's corruption; so that they might be pure and bright, for dust and grime signify illness and suffering; so that they might become obedient and harmonious, for in the heavens there is neither rebellion nor chaos...

So pass the hours of the night. The sleepy world inhales this restorative wisdom, the air becomes pure and blessed, colors become enlivened and beautiful, flowers grow gently and gratefully fragrant, the birds and animals hearken to the harmony of the heavens through their dreams.

This is why a person can be so joyful when he rises in the early hours and takes part in the awakening of the healed world, when he takes a breath of the cleansed air and sees nature renewed, hears the rejoicing of the feathered creatures, bids farewell to the fading stars, and feels the very breath of God in the newborn day, the rising sun and its first wonderfully cool emanation. Then he begins his day as if he had been reborn for the purpose of living: his heart has been cleansed and his will is alive with hopes; his vision has been renewed, and his thoughts have been opened...

Every day brings us that blessed early hour, for every morning is *God's morning*, but we forget this and go through life passing God's grace by, not knowing how to find it or treasure its gifts.

About Age

Is a person ever content with what he has been given? He always wants something else—to be someone else, to have more, to do what he does not know how to do. He never has enough! He always complains, and claims that he deserves more. He doesn't know how to appreciate what he has or how to make the best of it; too often it seems to him that he must obtain the things he doesn't have. We are all insatiable and ungrateful people, prone to complaining and discontent. It is the same way with age...

There is a dividing line in a person's life. Before it he hurries the passage of time; after it he would like to slow time, or stop it completely. People cross this line at varying points in their lives. *Before* it a person says to himself and others, "Well, I am not that young," because it seems to him that he is being treated like a child. Yet *after* it a person is always ready to say to others, as well as to himself, "Well, I am not that old yet," because he feels the burden of his years and does not wish to succumb to it. We all secretly look askance at others, wondering what they think of us, how receptive they are to us, and how old they think we are. Meanwhile these "others," who were never taught fair discernment of people, determine age according to external indicators, yet these indicators are all too often deceiving. A person's essence is defined by his internal state of being, which is not reflected by external indicators. Age, specifically, relates to the inner world of a person, for it is a spiritual quality.

Some children have no heart or imagination; they are calculating beyond their years and callous from birth, "a barren harvest, ripened before its time."[16] They were never young and came into the world as withered old men, while some people of advanced years

---

[16] M.I. Lermontov.

with profound heart and a living spirit resemble a noble old fiery wine. He whose heart sings is eternally young, but he whose heart has never sung was born an old man. True youth is an attribute of the *spirit* and its strength, its creativity. Wherever the spirit moves and blossoms, wherever the heart sings—there, old age is merely the tactlessness of time and a phantom reality. Unfortunately, people don't know much about this. They do not have enough spiritual strength to determine their own age, and they lack the skill of remaining spiritually young. For this reason they succumb to the state of their bodies, anxiously count the years that have passed, helplessly watching their thinning hair, trying to hide their true age from everyone, taking offense at indelicate questions, and keeping quiet about their birthdays. In the end, their glands become the most important thing in their lives... Too often we are unhappy because of our nearsightedness and naiveté; we don't understand that *spirituality is the key* to true happiness...

In his youth, a person looks ahead and anticipates future opportunities. He cannot wait to become a little older and prove himself an adult, for everywhere he hears offending words—"child," "little boy," "milksop"—and is convinced that people are exchanging smiles on his account. He dreams of emerging from his childhood years, in order to take part in all the secrets of adulthood that have been hidden from him, for some reason... Why?

And so it happens: the trials of childhood end and the adults talk with him as with a fellow adult; his boyish sensitivity goes away; he has no more youthful arrogance or peevishness. But now it seems to him that the older generation is dull and tiresome, that there is something old-fashioned, overdone, even dried up and withered about it. "These old men" think that they have some sort of "life experience," which he supposedly lacks; they think they all know and understand things better than he, and wish that everything should remain "as before, just like mother did it." They all look to their own authority and never allow him a chance. Well, at least time is passing, and soon he will come into his own...

Without even noticing, he steps over that fateful line—that parting of the waters of life—after which a person stops rushing forward and comes to his senses, but only when it is all over and too late. No longer does he want to become older and older; it is enough. To the contrary, how nice it would be to slow down or even stop the flight of time. The younger generation, with its new tastes, manners, and perceptions, is growing up. And now it seems to him that these young people are somehow strange: there is something the matter with them, they don't even know what they want. "It is difficult to talk to them—they neither understand us, nor we them..." Soon he regrets the past; he would like to gain it back, to shed the weight of ten or fifteen years from his shoulders. But, alas, this is impossible...

And so man is never content, and incorrectly so, especially when it comes to age. We must never complain or grumble, hurry or delay; instead we must *separate ourselves* from our age and never succumb to it. Age is not determined by length of life or condition of the body; it is determined by other factors. There is no place here for submission or helplessness. It is demeaning to be afraid and make false pretenses. We must instead seek and attain *independence* from our age. We must not argue with it or grow weary because of it. Let old age come: it does not have to put an end to our youth. It is possible to be old and young at the same time. We must spiritually overcome our age and render it an irrelevant detail of our existence.

Easy to say... But how can it be done?

This is how.

First, we must calculate our age not according to the condition of our bodies, but according to the *condition of the spirit.* Secondly, in every stage of life, we must *take pleasure in its noblest joys* and resolve the spiritual tasks presented by that particular stage. Thirdly, at every age, we must live for the things that do not age and *do not grow old*—the things that have existed since the beginning of time and will exist for the rest of time. All of this is part of the art of living.

Every stage of life has its blooms. Each one brings its joys. Each one contains its own spiritual beauty. And we must take pleasure in all of these things.

The child opens his eyes and sees the world before him in all its wealth and glory. Every blade of grass is ready to tell him its secret, every flower looks at him with a tender welcome; every dragonfly charms him with its flight; every tree whispers to him of might and strength. This is a time of effortless wealth, wonder, joy, trust, and mystery; a time for the soul's virginal acceptance of everything, a creative seriousness in play, an immediate union with nature, and the spirit's first waking moments...

The youth discovers love in all its sweet agony, its tormenting bliss. Every woman seems to him a vessel of gentle mystery; she holds for him the promise of ideal, possible, impending happiness. This is the time for dreaming and searching, being timid and in love, forming friendships and being rejected; a time for questions with no answers, a time for struggling internally with his own self. Spring, chaste love, first storms, the first hardening of character through disappointments, the joy of sincere love for all creation...

The adult finds his life calling and takes his place in the world. An array of valuable and joyful discoveries awaits him. He comes to know life with all its difficulties, gravity, and responsibilities; he establishes his spiritual independence; he becomes convinced that a man's will is a formative and defining power. This is the time for the fine-tuning of his character, the discovery of his own strengths and abilities; it is a time for absorbing plans and prospects, a time for entering into marriage, for the birth of his first child. The time for joy in a newborn life, the joy of a love realized.

The mature man comes to know the joy and torment of human creativity and the significance of the divine in the world. He already sees both the veritable depth of life and the limits of his own strength. Before his eyes the true nature of things is revealed, and his life enters a period of productivity. This is the time for publishing the fruits of his labor, for educating a new generation, a time of merit, recognition, and ascent. This stage of life has the beauty of late summer with its fragrance of bales of hay and gathered apples; it is the joy of a complete and mature being.

Old age partakes of rest and peace of the heart. The old man sees before him the wondrous horizons of life, taking pleasure in the power of a willful renunciation. This is the time for delayed contemplation, sweet remembrances, and a developed spiritual maturity. It is a time of miraculous dispassion in friendship; the blessed wealth of autumn; the lonely watch on the guard tower; the wise man's quiet teaching; the philosopher's grief over the world; the hermit's prayer over the suffering of man.

The ancient elder is given even greater and higher things, however: he sees the mysterious purpose of the world in all its depth and nobility; he has already set his sights on the afterlife and is ready to put a cross on his time on the earth. It is a time of quiet liberation from everything that is overtly human in nature, for calm and self-denying contemplation, for blessing others through his love; it is a radiant sunset, the foretaste of an approaching life transformation.

Just think of it: man is happy if he has accepted the joys of old age and has not squandered the gifts of his youth. He is so happy if his heart is alive with song as before, while a child's sincerity shines in his elderly eyes...

And if he has led his life in service to the eternal—in love, in spiritual contemplation, and within the divine tapestry of the world—then his life was blessed and joyful... This means that he rejoiced in the breath of God in the world as a child; as a youth, he contemplated the divine spark in his beloved; entering into life, he already realized by Whom he was designed—and for what. As a mature man, he was firmly convinced of Who and what held claim on his loyalty. His wisdom in later life will be imbued with spiritual love, and he will illumine the people in his life like a spiritual beacon. He who steps into the ray of his light will feel its otherworldly source. And once he has left this world, he will peacefully and joyfully enter that eternal world to which his thoughts had already belonged his entire life...

If we live in *this* way, then our life will become a blooming garden. Age will be overcome, old age will become exalted... And there will no reason to grumble or complain.

III. THE GIFT OF PRAYER

About Spiritual Blindness

This is a common occurrence: when a person is deprived of something, it hurts him to see others who have it. "No one should have what I don't have." It is unpleasant to admit to himself that he is deprived and overlooked. Other people's advantages sting and offend him; only rarely does someone "forgive" others their endowments. Feelings of hurt and ill will towards someone turn so easily into envy and malice... But if the overlooked envier is given power over others, perhaps even unlimited power over others, then his own mediocrity may become completely unbearable for him. He will do everything he can to take away the "intolerable" and "unforgivable" advantages of those subject to him. Historically, situations like these have more than once ended in tragic conflict between the tyrants and the endowed.

If we listen to what today's militant atheists say, we will get the impression that we must begin to heed these raging preachers— preachers of atheism—who are trying to draw people to a new religion. And it truly is a religion—a religion of faithlessness and godlessness. The fact of the matter is not only that these people have eliminated any connection to God, but they also view their godlessness as their greatest achievement, as a liberating truth, as joyful news—or in a word, as a *new revelation*... Such an impression is not accidental; it is historically grounded and true. And he who considers this revelation of the new age will experience profound sorrow and dismay.

This sorrow at first resembles the painful feeling we experience when we see a person who is deaf or blind. We see an unfortunate human being who is deprived of a precious and wonderful organ that could have enriched and enlightened his soul. This organ reveals to us so much in the world; it gives us—those who can see and hear—such a wealth of life experience, such a flow of meaningful, profound, and pure feelings, that we cannot even imagine ourselves without it. A unique and intrinsically valuable appreciation for the world and its objects is revealed before our eyes, and this appreciation gives us an endless bounty of light and joy. Then, suddenly, we see people who are deprived of these organs and who apparently do not even suspect what we receive from them and experience through them. Needless to say, a glimpse of such people fills us with emotion, with mixed feelings of sympathy, great sorrow, and confusion.

This closely resembles what we feel when we first encounter a spiritually blind atheist on our life journey. How does he experience the world without God? What does he see in nature, how does he imagine the human soul? How does he deal with life's suffering and temptations? In what does he perceive the purpose and destiny of man? The world must seem to him completely dead, vapid, and trite; the fate of the human race must seem pointless, blind, and cruel.

Then a dim feeling of responsibility, perhaps even guilt awakens in us: we are happy, he is unhappy; we were given a wealth of spiritual gifts, of which he is deprived; we can perceive and see that he is blind. We must help him. What have we done to help him? What must we do to restore in his soul the organ of the spirit? What can we do for such people? And can we remain at peace with their impending spiritual doom?

Then suddenly we realize he has never noticed his own blindness and does not consider himself blind: on the contrary, he is very happy that he lacks that wonderful organ, that spiritual ability to contemplate, to see, to believe. He has no desire to obtain it. Instead, he perceives his deprivation as the beginning of a "new" life and new work, as a sign of a "higher calling," as the right to power and preaching. This beggar sees himself as a rich man; this dangerously ill man imagines that he, in particular, is a person of exemplary health; he thinks that he is a new being, destined for a great future. He is an "enlightened thinker," and we are the ones who are lost in darkness; if we are not deceived, then we are "malicious deceivers." And for this reason he must enlighten us, liberate us, and show us the way to a new and true happiness. In short, he is born to rule, and we are predestined for submission.

We realize then that everything is distorted; everything is turned inside out and upside down. We feel slightly dizzy. This sometimes happens when we are fast asleep; we dream what we later call nightmares where people walk backwards and fall not down, but up; where great riches are made of garbage and broken bits and pieces; where we are blind, and happy and proud because of it; where we are evil vermin, but still plan to rule the world... Finally, we wake up and thank God that these dreams are over...

This is what we feel when we listen to the preaching of modern atheists. Our feeling of compassion quickly disappears, giving way to surprise and outrage. Before us we see people who are confident and exacting to the highest degree, yet foolishly perceive their spiritual paucity as the highest gift and their commonplace visions as a new "revelation." They consider us backward, "obscurantist," enslaved to prejudice and superstition; they declare us to be their enemies and enemies of the life of the people; they give us the choice to either "rethink our views" and agree with them, or face torture and death. They tell us something like this: "We, the atheists, do not see any God, and do not wish to know anything about Him. This is wonderful—it is the beginning of a new freedom. And if this is blindness, then let everyone be blind like we are. Only then will everyone be set free, and our new life will begin. There is no God for us, and none of the rest of you dare believe in Him. Learn from us, for it is our destiny to teach and lead. But if you don't agree with us, we will slowly destroy you, until there are no believers left on this earth…"

We well know what happens when the blind lead the blind: both fall into a pit. But it is unheard of for the blind to start leading those who can see. It would be impossible for us to answer them with pity or compassion. In this case feelings of responsibility and indignation take precedence. We must stand in defense of right and restore the natural order of things. Of course, we cannot forbid the atheists their atheism; to forbid them will neither help them nor render them harmless. Freedom of religion includes freedom of unbelief. One should never be pushed either to unbelief or to faith. A person can only turn to God and come to believe in Him of his own accord. On the other hand, we must accept the atheists' challenge and give them a worthy answer. We must calmly, objectively, and decisively prove to them that we do not need their "enlightenment," for we already see the spiritual light. This light has already liberated us, and thus our faith is objective and free in nature; because through its activity it liberates us with its strength and its essence, *we need no liberation from this freedom*. We must say that the atheists' new, imaginary "revelation" is in truth blindness, self-deception, and darkness; it gives them no right to power, but leads instead to death.

We, who believe in God, are not blind in the least. We see everything that the atheists see, but we interpret and evaluate it in a completely different way. Moreover, in addition to what they see, we see something *else* that is invariably more important, precious, profound, and sacred than what they see. However, we should not be labeled as "hypocrites" or "daydreamers" because of this.

It would be better not to speak of hypocrisy at all, for hypocrites can be found in every direction or trend. The very existence of these impostors says nothing against the existence of Truth or Object. We should consider only sincere people and honest thinkers.

Neither do we accept the title of daydreamer. The daydreamer looks into emptiness, composes stories about things that don't exist, and believes in the fictions of his own imagination. We, on the contrary, have a living relationship with *actual existing realities*; we don't need to make things up or to sow the emptiness with our myths. What we see can never be attributed to hallucination. Hallucination is a trick of the sense of sight, but our senses remain sober, natural, and healthy; they suffer neither ecstasy nor deceit. He who hallucinates is insane: he sees sensory dreams in real life, keeps company with illusions, and accepts them as material fact. We, however, are free of all this. We are not madmen or fools; we experience the world in the same way as other healthy people, without distorting it through illusions or dreams. Among men of faith, there have been more than a handful of brilliant scientists and inventors: Copernicus, Roger Bacon, Francis Bacon, Galileo, Kepler, Leibniz, Boyle, von Liebig, Rudolf Mayer, Schleiden, Du-Bois Reymond, Fechner, and many others. Did they not create the laws of positivism? When or where did they ever deal with objectless fantasies or give way to hallucinations? These were sober-minded observers, keen researchers, responsible thinkers, and great masters of Objectivity. And yet they believed in God; they openly professed their faith. On what grounds did they acknowledge God? Why? Because their *contemplative experience* opened to them not only the material world of the physical senses, but also the great *capacity of the spirit* and its realities.

True faith does not arise from subjective frames of mind or random constructions. It develops from vast experience and is always rooted in an objective contemplation of the spirit. This spiritual experience deals with realities not of a sensory nature (the conscience), not limited to the senses (art), or simply of a supersensory nature (religion). This experience is neither daydream nor insanity. It demands *spiritual sobriety* and lends itself to *spiritual examination*. It has its preparations, its purification and special exercises; it is materialized in objective perception and realized through total and conclusive evidence. And he who prematurely rejects this, desiring to know nothing about it, has neither the right nor the foundation to criticize faith and reject religion.

What can a blind person say about the colors of a beautiful painting or an exquisite flower? Nothing! And yet some would conclude from this that the painting doesn't exist at all, or that this flower is our hallucination... Who will believe the deaf man who announces that there is no such thing as music, that it is nothing but "a fiction of hypocrites?" A person who is deprived of the spiritual eye and ear has no grounds or right to speak of spiritual subjects. A person with a callous heart or deadened spiritual perception knows nothing of *love*, for how can he perceive God's love? Does he dare reject it and blasphemously ridicule it? A person who lives without moral judgment and knows nothing of the strength and bliss of the conscience-driven act will have not the slightest idea of good and evil, sin and mercy, God's goodness and redemption... How can we explain to him what *prayer* is? How will he believe that prayer is accepted and heard? How can he be sure that true faith never arises out of fear, but is designed to *overcome every fear*? How can we explain to a person who knows neither the spirit nor freedom that faith in God *frees the spirit*, while the atheism he preaches only brings *the greatest enslavement* history has ever seen—enslavement to the passions, material things, and godless tyrants?

Yes, true faith holds company with the greatest and most wonderful of realities which awaken man's worthiest creative efforts. Communicating with these realities, people of faith are freed from their overly human fears and do not give way to such fears —even when they are waging battle for the sake of holy endeavors in life, or when they must choose the path of confession and martyrdom. At such times their fear is overcome by the power of the spirit, and they leave this life victorious. Today's atheists, with their persecution of religion, have certainly seen this countless times.

These great and illuminating realities are never obtained in some impenetrable and terrible darkness, as the atheists imagine.

God does not live only on this side of our physical world. He is also present there, on the "other side." He gives people His light and pours forth His strength. He gives of Himself and reveals Himself to us, while we are able to and called upon to receive His life-giving breath and His will at all times and in all things. Wherever nature or human culture discovers something wonderful, true, or complete, there the Spirit of God breathes: in the mysterious wonder of a crystal, in the organic flowering of nature, in love, in the heroic deed, in the visual arts, in scientific thought, in the conscience-driven act, in worldly justice, in legal freedom, in inspired government, in contemplative labor, in the simple human kindness shining in a person's eyes... And where we are gathered together in His name and pray to Him, there He is in the midst of us...

And when the atheists ask us why we don't see Him with our *physical eye*, we answer that it is precisely because we do not hallucinate. We perceive Him not with our body, not with our senses, but with our spirit, through our spiritual experience, and with our spiritual vision. It is pointless, naïve, and primitive to imagine that the only realities are those accessible through our five senses.

Just as the world would never have been created without God, so all of human culture will fall apart if God should ever abandon it. There would be no life without the sun; the human spirit cannot survive without God. If man is denied and abandoned by God, he lays his creative potential to waste: he becomes a heartless, uninspired, ruthless creature, powerless to contemplate and create new, complete forms, capable only of sharing his torment and destroying everything. His life becomes filled with fear, penal labor, and continued betrayal. History has already witnessed this enough— is further proof or more suffering really necessary? He who preaches godlessness prepares people for a path of great adversity: dissolution, mortification, slavery, and torment...

The mission of our generation is to show people their terrible impending fate, to convince them that any path without God leads to destruction… And yet how can we show this fate to the spiritually blind, who neither see nor desire to see?

The Mountain Lake

Far from the well-trodden public roads, high up at the foot of a steep cliff, rests a mountain lake submerged in its own thoughts. It peers up with a pure eye into the world's expanse, taking in everything that the heavens send its way, obediently and clearly reflecting in itself the heavens' gifts… It is the earth's mirror of events in the heights…

It is not easy to reach. The ascent is long, and one must travel patiently step by step, higher and higher, with the firm hope of seeing something extraordinary. The climb becomes more difficult, the environment more strict and sparse, the brisk air more cool. All around, the chaos is stilled. The cliffs are overgrown with a deep moss. The whispers of the rare firs are barely heard. A primeval, sacred silence reigns. Two blue butterflies, blithely celebrating their happiness, chase each other through the bright expanse.

Then, suddenly, the traveler feels *its* presence. He cannot yet see it, but his soul is seized with a certainty that his journey has come to an end, and that he will see it at any moment. This complete, reverent stillness is a sure sign of its proximity; this light, slightly humid, beckoning breeze can only come from it; he can feel, somewhere close by, a certain living focal point, around which and for the sake of which exists everything that surrounds it… And here *it* is, at last, in all of its quiet magnificence.

Its banks are simple and stern; it needs no scenery, seeks no ornament. It lies openly, to see everything and to everything give reply. Its clear waters are still; its surface appears perfectly smooth. Its depths gently glimmer in countless elusive shades of varying blue and green; it is perfectly translucent to the very bottom. There, in the depths, he can see fallen mountains so deep that the eye doubts the distance; he sees hundred-year-old trunks of trees—the submerged gifts of the mountains, a whole world of happily welcomed and preserved treasures, a world of blissful existence. It all rests there like a clear dream, forever treasured, an eternal remembrance; like the fruits of a first profound contemplation; like the wordless prayers of the ascetic. And little by little, the soul begins to understand the reason for this wondrous stillness all around, why there are no mountain voices to be heard, why even the birds do not sing and the newly arrived travelers begin to speak to each other in whispers. Nature knows how to guard its secrets and preserve that sacred silence. And it demands the same of people. Wherever the Divine rests, there is heard the silent passing of centuries.

The traveler walks around the lake, then suddenly stops in amazement. Everything that he could see before in the depths has vanished. In its stead has appeared a new and stately image of breathtaking beauty, a mountain ridge complete with crags and gorges, snow and ice, scattered groups of clouds, all in the rays of the sun, all shining, miraculously inverted, as if projected onto the glassy water. Is it an apparition? But this apparition doesn't vanish; it stays, remaining and radiating joy and light... Perhaps this is just a game of the sunbeams on the water. Perhaps... But this game makes the heart tremble with joy: it both believes and doubts this sight; it hears a hymn to God; it feels the wisdom and beauty of the universe and awaits in suspense any further visions of light and depth.

Overwhelmed and joyful, the traveler stands at the shore; he sees and yet doubts his own eyes, wanting more and more to make certain of it and ingrain the sight into his memory. He looks until his heart, overflowing with joy and gratitude, demands rest, and his tired eyes dim with tears. Only then does he sit down on the nearest rock to rest.

When the day's light dims and dusk quietly falls, when the first stars appear and the crescent arrives from behind a steep mountain—what joy it is to seek and find all these images in the darkened depths of the lake! Now these depths are no longer translucent; they have withdrawn into themselves; the blackened water lies mysteriously and heavily still, and in this black glass the moonlight is magically conjured up. Later, the traveler hardly remembers how he reached shelter that night or where he slept until very morning. And yet there everything has already awoken, and rejoices in the dawn of God…

How breathtaking are those first submerged riches of the transparent lake, its own eternal thoughts! With what simplicity and dignity, what clarity and sincerity, does it reveal the depth of its being, initiating every person into its mysteries. Oh, the purity of the heart! Oh clear, generous wisdom!

But how magnificent, how blinding are its reflected visions! Its smooth surface accepts these gifts so faithfully, and so willingly and joyfully gives them back to every eye… It takes joy in all things that come from the Father of Light: the blue sky, the barely visible stars, the dreaming evening cloud, the ascending bare cliff, every tree, every peak—all things that in turn have the joy of gazing back into it. It shares this joy with every new guest, every weary traveler, who comes up and reverently looks into its depths. No one will leave without an answer, and everyone will take away comfort, light, and love of life… Oh, the humility of the spirit! Oh, the contemplation of peace! Oh, the joy of service!

So it rests in its simple and somber setting, this eye of the world, accepting and treasuring God's gifts, just like the righteous man who seeks only heavenly visions and strictly observes purity and transparency of heart for their sake. Two worlds meet in the lake—the internal world of sacred thoughts and the external world of God-given visions—which join together into a single, bright, and generous wealth of wisdom.

The Return

Modern mankind is experiencing a time of great turmoil. The fundamentals of life are falling apart. Spiritual foundations have become hazy. A great collapse is upon us, with threats of more and more tribulation. In the midst of the adversity and suffering of our time, the temptations inundating us and the fears surrounding us, we learn to pray once again. For we have lost this highest of gifts and have forgotten this wonderful skill. And yet without prayer, man finds himself fallen away from God, torn from the source of true life: he has been surrendered to the origin of evil and has no strength to fight it.

All people, no matter who they are or what they do in life—whether man or woman, old or young, educated or uneducated—must be able to collect their spiritual strength and concentration. This is the first goal of every upbringing, beginning in the village schools and ending with university-level education. Life flows by and through us in a stream of every possible kind of feeling, desire, and passion—a multitude of various cares and occupations, a cloud of dust consisting of fragmented and insignificant contents. We lose ourselves in this flow, this fog, and we lose the meaning of our lives. We are seized and overcome by petty trifles that have no higher purpose. The dust of life darkens our vision and deprives us of our sight. We are sucked into a bog of passions, especially conceit and greed. It is imperative that we free ourselves from all of this, be it only from time to time. We cannot die in this swamp. We should not give in to this current. We need to set aside minutes, or even hours, for unrestricted breathing and contemplation, for a time when all our cares are silenced, when everything that makes up our daily life is forgotten and we free ourselves from every trifling, overly human, and vulgar thing. Our spiritual powers—our thoughts, desires, feelings, and imagination—are delivered from the petty and trivial; they search for something different and better; they turn inward and concentrate on what makes up the very essence of our being; on what is most important in a person's life; on what is *sacred and illuminating* and determines the very purpose of our existence. This is the first step toward prayer.

If I am able to completely step away from the quotidian and chaotic content of my life, then my heart and will become open to the best and most exalted things. But what are these "best" things? How can I find these "most exalted" things? How do I recognize them? And why do I ask these questions, as if I knew nothing about these things? Can it be that I have lived so many years on this earth without ever posing these questions to myself? Or, if I did ask myself these questions, was I unable to answer them? Then how did I live before today, if I never knew the sacred and illuminating, if I am unable to bring them to life within myself? What occupies my daily life so much? How is it illuminated, if not by this light? How is it blessed, if not by this sanctity? How is it justified, if this basic purpose is not given to me even in moments of freedom and concentration? These questions lead my soul into confusion and dismay; the soul sees the emptiness of its existence and the triviality of its makeup, and responds with a holistic impulse toward the good, toward the sacred, illuminating things that make sense of life. In this impulse it understands that such things can only be *perfect*, intrinsically perfect, and furthermore neither fantastical nor illusory; they are an *intrinsically tangible, true ideal*. That is how a living desire for God, and the desire to be near Him, is born. For God is an intrinsically tangible ideal, and a living and holistic impulse towards Him is the *prayer* that has sprung forth.

Prayer is a concentrated, earnest appeal to the Supreme Being. Turning to Him, appealing to Him, we open our souls to Him; then, our opened souls then rise up to Him and enter into a living, creative union with Him. This is the essence of every prayer—the wisest prayer and the most naïve prayer, the wordless prayer and the abundantly worded prayer, the prayer of supplication and the prayer of gratitude—to the extent that people of all religions are able to pray together as one.

But our Christian prayer is not defined in this way. For we appeal not to an intangible, mysterious, and impersonal Ideal, but to a living, perfect God, to our Heavenly Father, Who, indivisible from the Son of God and the Holy Spirit, listens to the prayers of His earthly children. We see in God first and foremost an inexhaustible *source of love*, which we approach on our own and emulate through that very same love. The fragile ray of our love finds His love, is strengthened and defined by it, and takes in the goodness and power emanating from it. In this way we are given three of the greatest comforts: a sense of immediate communion with God; the feeling that our prayer may be heard by Him; and the feeling that He knows us, loves us, and watches over us. The Christian who finds God through love and sees that God responds to him and his love with His own Love, is inherently certain that he cannot be abandoned by God, that he is forever in the palm of His loving hand and in the shelter of His gracious protection. And so the Christian prays first and foremost *with his heart*, with an open and sincere heart; he surrenders himself to the will of his loving Father. This is precisely why it is essential and imperative for us, living as we do in this current era of ruin, temptations, dangers, and fears, to find His shelter, His help, His light, and His power.

But in addition to this, we must observe two basic requirements. We should not imagine that we can appeal to the God of love and light in every one of our worldly doings and schemes, for our earthly actions are sometimes crude and selfish, and often nefarious, insidious, and destructive. We cannot call upon the God of light in our dark and soulless undertakings. We should not expect help from the God of love in predatory and hateful matters. Prayer is only justified and purposeful in the battle for good.

If my aim is indeed good, or one that can be justified in the face of His love and perfection, then I can boldly and confidently request His help. The first help that I can beseech is the enlightenment and illumination of my soul in matters of choice and service: that I be given the ability to faithfully discern between good and evil, and unfailingly desire goodness and perfection; that I be given pure contemplation, reliable insight, true perception, and firm decision. I need to be sure that I have truly come to recognize His work and am truly serving Him with my love and my will. If I can be sure, then I can ask for help, pray with "confidence" (1 John 5:14), and quietly hope: "Help me in the service of Your work…" He who listens to the voice of his Christian conscience prays with great assurance, for he prays together with, out of, and for the sake of, his conscience.

The Stoic Aulus Persius Flaccus, a famous Roman satirist of the pagan era, writes that people often ask of the gods things so base, regarding matters so pitiful and foul, that they would never dare whisper these things except to their closest friends. Such prayer is not only blasphemous (for it seeks to find in God a participant in dark doings), but it is also useless, for we cannot direct it to the God of light and love. We should not utter these words in prayer: "Lord, help me in my base and nefarious undertakings; grant me success in my criminal actions, and crown my sins with victory and happiness." He who utters such a prayer prays not to God but to his lord, the devil.

That is the first requirement of true prayer. But there is also a second one.

No prayer excludes my own efforts or renders them futile: my love, my desire, my effort, and my struggle must all be dedicated to that matter about which I pray. If that matter is indeed good and true before the face of God, then I must dedicate to it even more effort—to serve it, fight for it, defy any threat, and meet every danger. Then my service itself becomes a prayer; then I pray together with my love, my will, my courage, and my good standing; then I am sure that I am serving God with all my strength and that my prayer will be heard. The Lord will open my spiritual eyes so that I can see truly and clearly; purify my heart so that I may sincerely love the ideal; strengthen my will so that I may not despair or grow weary on my journey; direct my steps so that I may not stray or take the false path. And even if *my* strength should fail, and even if all of our human powers should prove lacking, then through our prayers the heavenly powers would make the impossible possible.

If I am praying for myself, for my life and wellbeing, then I should be certain that I am walking on my life's true path. A prayer sprung forth from a pure conscience can cause wonders. He who sacrifices himself in battle for the sake of God's cause may call upon God with great boldness. He who lays aside his own concerns for the sake of God's work feels loved and protected; he prays to God like a beloved child who appeals to his loving father: "Oh Lord, do not leave Your child helpless. Teach and protect Your faithful son." Thus true prayer forms and rises up to God. Such prayer is a spiritual skill in itself, and we must put this skill to use within ourselves in the face of the great troubles besetting us. Every fear and misfortune of our time, every spiritual upheaval that we now experience in the revolutions and wars of our days—all of this is a great cleansing of our souls, a lesson in faith and prayer.

About Prayer

The human spirit knows no comfort more effective or pure than prayer. It brings a person purification and strength, tranquility and joy, blessing and healing. He who has never experienced this should not pass judgment on prayer, for he has yet to obtain its consolation in his struggles and suffering. Then he will feel that he has entered into communion with a new source of life, that a new existence has begun within him—one which before he could never have imagined.

The life of modern man is filled with eternal cares and anxieties ranging from disappointment to illness, from personal sorrow to shared adversity. He knows neither what to undertake nor how to survive all this; at times he is filled with horror at the thought that this dismal torrent will carry him away and pour down upon him to his very death. At the same time, in reality, his fate is in his own hands: he himself increases his own burden in life, and yet he cannot make sense of the weight that he carries. For his path has already been revealed to him: it is up to him to realize his *spiritual freedom* and open his spiritual eyes. This happens through prayer.

We would all like to see our ungainly, oppressive, and often demeaning lives begin again and unfold differently, to bloom in shared confidence, inspiration, and a sincere desire for universal wellbeing. However, we don't know how to make this happen. With our short-sighted logic, we speak of "happiness," which, unnoticed by us, evolves into "pleasure" and "enjoyment" in our lives. As a result, we wander into a swamp and don't know what to do next. But the path that leads to our life's renewal is well-known and fairly simple: we must *feel the sacred* in our lives through the heart, concentrating on it within our contemplation and living by it as something sacred and all-important. This is the path to prayer.

We must not drown in the inessential things of life. He who lives by such things finds himself accustomed to vulgar living and so becomes, according to Gogol, an "exister."[17] Thus, it is essential for us to learn how to accurately determine *the spiritual level of every aspect of our lives,* and then train ourselves to focus our inner attention on the divine essence of things, occurrences, and events. For the things that make up our lives are never equal in nature, of equal value, or equally significant. They include things both trivial and sacred; things that elevate the soul and introduce it to great depth and power as well as things that invisibly decay and weaken it, rendering it pitiful, passionate, and blind. There are things that are worth living for, and things that are not. We must learn to identify them, to choose the worthy and the sacred from among them, and live for their sake. Then the person will himself become "worthy:" he will understand the purpose and meaning of life and enter into a living communion with the sacred essence of the visible world. The path leading to this ability is revealed through and forged by prayer.

We should never think that taking the first steps on this path is not within our power, or that extremely difficult times complicate a prayerful renewal of our lives, or that the authority of

---

[17] *Translator's note:* Gogol was troubled by the lack of spiritual depth in his peers, whom he dubbed the "existers."

men in the world can deprive a person of his inner freedom and enslave him to the immaterialities of existence. In truth, these difficult times are given to us specifically as a chance to come to our senses and restore our lives. There is no earthly power strong enough to extinguish our inner freedom—or more importantly, *the freedom to pray*—or to prevent our deliverance from depravity.

This is why we must admit that life is in itself a *school for prayer*, an education in prayer. And even he who has never prayed can be brought to prayer by life itself. For in the life of every man— even one who does not believe—can come a time of great woe, when the shocked and startled heart suddenly begins to pray from its last remaining depths in such sorrowing helplessness, with such sighs of despair, such inspired appeals, the likes of which he could never have imagined. Then he will experience something like an earthquake in his entire being, and an invisible flame will engulf his soul. It may even be that the person does not know to whom he appeals; he cannot imagine what sort of salvation might come to him, or from where. He calls on Someone who can do *anything*, even the impossible; he begs this Unknown Being for help which surpasses human ability, pleading with the firm belief that there *is* a true Good on earth and that It hears him. And to this unknown but almighty Good he turns in prayer, and his prayer, like a flood of water, abruptly breaks through all his previously constructed dams. He begins to speak to this Being as if he saw Him standing before him, as if he had known Him since the beginning of time…

And then, when this impulse passes, he still has a feeling that he has always believed in this All-Good, Almighty Being, and has always assumed His presence with every breath; now, he has simply found Him for the first time. What he previously lacked was *a spiritual ascent toward inspired prayer*. He needed a courageous heart in order to defy his own and others' preconceptions; integrity of soul, brought about by his present instinctual despair; wisdom of heart, which would have emerged victorious over any foolishness of the mind; and inspiration, which never comes to a soul covered in dust and grime. Perhaps he had already noticed this himself, for he felt both fragmented and whole. Perhaps he was even tormented by it, but could not and would not overcome this internal division, thus forbidding himself to pray under the pretense of his intrinsic honor. This state reveals the general influence of our time, which "believes" in the mind and in analysis, and cultivates every possible decon-struction… And only the great troubles of our time can give us the ability to overcome these internal obstacles, for these troubles shake our very foundations, washing away all preconceptions, exposing our trembling emotional core, and transforming our lives into a veritable school of prayer.

The fact is that true prayer requires the *entire* person and seizes him whole. A person can pray in a stream of connected words, but he can also find himself at a loss for words, able only to call out in tears, like Holy Andrew the Fool for Christ: "Lord!! Lord!! Lord!!" And this one heartfelt word will carry greater weight than a multitude of spiritually half-empty words. Prayer may find expression in devout gestures and rites, but in some prayers external movement and action are eliminated altogether. A heavily wounded man cannot even cross himself; a person lying motionless in a trench dares not even flinch. And people living in an age of persecution of faith, a time of terror within the Church, develop the ability to form an *internal prayer of the heart,* which burns with an inner fire underneath a completely motionless and expressionless outward appearance.

This fire of internal prayer is the most important and most precious thing in religion. It requires a person's entire soul. In this fire every color comes together to form a white light; all the abilities of the soul form a unified force. St. Theophan the Recluse describes this condition as "the man who is whole must be on fire."[18] Here thoughts do not think, analyze, ponder, or doubt; they give up their force, their intensity, to the common and unified flame. There are

---

[18] *Translator's note:* St. Theophan the Recluse. *The Path to Salvation.*

no separate willful decisions, but only a unified flowing *force of will* directed in its entirety at a single Object. The heart with its profound and gentle emotional core becomes the foundational rock of the soul; within it is concentrated the power of contemplation, which issues forth from it and returns back again.

That is why prayer is, in a sense, the *heart's heat*, absorbing everything into itself and then melting and liquefying it. It is a certain spiritual light, gathering rays like a magnifying glass into a single center—and in this center a flame bursts out. The inexperienced person often feels that this flame is his own subjective, limited state. In truth, this flame leads the individual's soul toward a supernatural Flame, which responds to the individual's plea and absorbs into Itself the individually burning heart. In prayer, a person's flame can and must commune with the Divine Flame; therein lies the mysterious meaning and blessed power of prayer. A person's heart is set aflame with the divine Fire and becomes like the Burning Bush. The individual's fire is integrated into the Divine Flame, and the person loses himself in His Fire. In true prayer, a person forgets and loses himself: he has already forgotten that he "is" and no longer has a sense of his own physical being; he imagines and feels that he is in a *pillar of fire* rising upward, and he hears "groanings which cannot be uttered" of "the Spirit itself" (Romans 8:26) issuing forth from his soul... And in this light and fire he is carried away as far as his heart and breath will take him.

Coming back to himself after such prayer, a person feels as if he has been deemed worthy to visit his native and sacred land, or rather, as if the very essence (substance) of his spiritual person had been renewed, as if a blessed stream of pure vision and knowledge, comfort, and peace had washed over him. He becomes convinced that true *good* and true *Power* is one and the same; he feels connected to this grace-filled power; he has drunk his fill of the source of life and love.

After such prayer (even if it lasted for only a minute), a certain inextinguishable, shining, living *coal* remains in the person's heart, spreading its luminescence throughout his soul's expanse, ever ready to burst into its own supernatural flame. In other words true prayer leaves behind a *quiet, mysterious, wordless prayerfulness,* like an unfading, tranquil, yet forceful light. It ceaselessly shines from the depths of the heart, as if desiring to illuminate and sanctify all the worldly contents of our soul. It is like the quiet breath of God issued from another world. It is like an altar door left ajar and leading us to the sacred place of God's presence. True prayer gives a person the wonderful feeling that the Otherworldly has become part of this world in his heart and conscience.

In the meantime life continues at its unstoppable pace, and it sometimes seems to the person that nothing unusual has happened, except that in him now dwells the radiance of his wordless, quietly reverent prayer, asking for nothing nor soliciting anything. He knows of this door to communion that has been opened for him, and knows that it leads to the font of healing water. Thus he is able to manage his daily affairs, to eat, drink, sleep, work hard, and give himself over to rest, while this internal light never leaves him: it fires up and cleanses his soul by measures, shining forth in all his worldly doings and illuminating in them the good and the evil, confirming him in goodness, and eliminating his ability to commit wicked, callous, base, and depraved acts. Such a person can forget about this coal of wordless prayer quietly smoldering within him, but this coal will elusively perform its great task—a task that will give life meaning, purifying, sanctifying, and healing. The person has but to knock on that door again, appealing to that light—and the flame will come to life again, the heart will break out in song, a living love will issue forth, a purified conscience will begin to speak, and the door leading to the other world with a view onto his eternal life will be revealed before his eyes. Once again he will feel that he is on the brink of earthly life, and he will hear the breath of God within himself and in the world.

Now, however, he knows that his first prayer of horror and despair, which he uttered in fear of perishing, was only a first helpless impulse, only the first step on his new path. Now he prays differently: he burns freely, radiates continuously, and includes his entire life in this prayer. These are the highest types of prayer. There are as many of them as the various actions a person can commit in life. "There are as many forms of prayer as possible spiritual states and moods in one soul, or in every soul."[19] There are prayers of gratitude, worship, humility, repentance, and absolution. A prayer may heed the breath of God, contemplate the wisdom of the Creator, and give clarity; a prayer may doubt, question, despair, grieve, or invoke. Copernicus prayerfully listened to the laws of nature. Fechner prayed together with the flowers and the trees. Segantini bowed down before mountains as if before the altars of God. Lomonosov prayed with the northern lights. Derzhavin prayed while contemplating the frailty of the world and the eternity of the Divine, Pushkin with every stroke of inspiration, Lermontov together with the lilies-of-the-valley by the stream. God gave man a great freedom in prayer—the freedom *to transform every action of his life and work into a fruitful prayer*, like that wonderful prayer of the sower introduced by Leskov in *The Cathedral Clergy*: "Lord, establish and multiply and grow a portion for every person, whether hungry and orphaned, wanting, imploring, allowing, thankful, or ungrateful...."

Similarly, there are prayers of exhaustion ("Lord, I cannot go on") that are uttered with many tears and which grant *strength*.

There are also wordless and tearless prayers, momentary, contemplative, and radiant, a single glance of the spiritual eye directed above: "He is, He is vigilant, and I am His instrument." This is a prayer of *comfort and strength*.

There are prayers from a warm heart, for example a prayer simply to approach His inextinguishable coal inside ourselves—that would be enough.

---

[19] St. John Cassian.

Finally, a prayer of *service and triumph* will always carry a defining weight on every path and in every suffering in the individual's life: "I stand before You, Lord, Your servant, seeking only Your will. Teach me to serve you faithfully, with every breath and act. Grant me Your strength, Your wisdom, Your inspiration. Do not surrender me to the abuse of Your enemies; deliver me from their threats. And preserve my freedom in life and in my work, for my freedom lies in the realization of Your will."

On these paths life becomes the school of prayer, and prayer becomes the true source of life and fruitful work.

About the World's Sorrow

It is truly one of the basic laws of our world that all beings and all things are imperfect, and they must rise to perfection through *battle and suffering.* The significance of this law for a person's life and work is so great, and so profound, that he truly matures only when he considers and realizes this law in his every conclusion and deduction. Everything good, significant, and eternal—especially what is ingenious and divine in human culture—could only have come out of suffering; the person must have done something to deserve it and to be able to make sense of it. This is what profound thinker and Czech mystic Jacob Boehme meant when he wrote that quality is born out of agony.[20]

Through comprehension of this law, we receive a certain grace-filled release from the spiritual helplessness that threatens everyone on earth. This comprehension extracts us from the murky stream of our life, lifting us above the suffering world for at least a moment to show it to us *from outside and from above.* And if hitherto a person lived like a creature among creatures, then henceforth he obtains the ability to leave the world in spirit, to see its anguish and question the meaning of its existence and suffering.

---

[20] "Die qualitat quillt aus der Qual."

Hitherto he only suffered in the world among creatures like he; henceforth he steps onto a higher plain of existence, for he becomes able to *suffer because of the suffering of the world*, i.e. to experience the world's sorrow.

All growing and living things suffer within the world, remaining within its confines and comprising its population, but it is not given to them to suffer *because* of the world or *for* the world. Man is given the higher gift of ascending above the created living world and to weep over the fate of all creation, to share in its suffering. Thus, man is called upon to conceive and understand that *all living things must suffer*. Man must listen to the sighs and moans of the universe, including those of human beings, and heed them with an open heart, joining the world's sorrow through selfless compassion. We as human beings must all take part in the torment and woe of grieving nature, and through this compassion forget our own suffering. We must take on the suffering of all living things and bear this burden as the common and unified cross of the world; we must try to comprehend the profound meaning of this universal cross. By doing so we give ourselves over to the world's sorrow, i.e., to suffering because of the world's suffering. And by surrendering itself to this sorrow, our spirit ascends and enters into a blessed nearness to God.

So long as a person is imprisoned and blinded by his own personal suffering, when he rushes about helplessly and sees no way out because of his own blindness, he is defeated by his brute nature and cannot find his way to God. He must come out of his own self in spirit, rise above himself, and see the suffering of his neighbor, of all people, of all created things. At first he will be horrified, and this horror in the face of the world's torment will lead to indignation, protests, and perhaps even rebellion. These feelings and moods will lead him not *to* God, but *away from God*, and may even urge him *against* God. For this blind indignation is a specific characteristic of the created being in relation to another created being; if he rises up against God, he does not free himself as a creature from his personhood but instead preserves his blindness, paving the way to bitterness and rendering himself an insurgent creature. A person blinded by horror can see neither distance nor depth; he resists light and reason and withdraws into disgust and rejection. A contemplation of the world's torment requires courage—a courage that he does not have. This contemplation should give him wings, but he remains wingless. A creature's fear leads him away into the dark vaults of hopelessness, pessimism, and rejection of God. In this darkness he is slowly taken over by artificial, aggressive "demonism" and a Satanism fueled by hatred and pride. Then his sorrow becomes godless, malicious, and destructive. This was the fate of every pessimistic philosophy and literature of the nineteenth century.

Only love can save a person and set him free. Its first and most basic form is sympathy for the suffering one. A person feels for someone else in his torment, sympathizes with him, and begins to demonstrate a living and constructive participation. He forgets about himself, living for the sake of the other person's suffering, and by doing so he frees himself from dwelling on his own pain and individual grief. His own personhood no longer binds nor blinds him; in its place someone else's personhood begins to overcome him, filling his life and soul. If he doesn't notice this in time to defeat this new prison, then he will soon become a prisoner of another creature's torment. As long as sympathy has the final say and remains the highest expression of his love, the suffering of any living being will seem to him a tragedy or misfortune, and he will see the existing "evil" in every creature's torment.[21] He begins to believe that the higher purpose of life lies in mankind's deliverance from suffering. He can no longer bear to see a suffering being, and the battle against suffering becomes his primary concern. A life without illness seems to him the highest earthly good.

---

[21] L.N. Tolstoy.

This signifies that the pitying person has *discovered his neighbor*, and this is very good. But he has not yet discovered the meaning of suffering; the purpose of humanity has not yet been revealed to him. His love for another person extends not to the "angel" hidden in the depths of the suffering soul who is fighting for liberation, but only to the sighing and crying creature; he undertakes not to help the "angel," but to serve the creature; his goal is not for the suffering spirit to be purified and emerge victorious, but to alleviate the created being's torment. This is why the pitying person is still weighed down by fear and horror, why he still renounces suffering and comprehends neither its meaning nor its grace: he is still afraid of pain and knows nothing of its enlightening nature nor the fruits of its defeat. And that is why the world's sorrow does not lead him to God: he remains within the confines of humanity and sentimentality, unreached by God's illuminating rays. Meanwhile, he does not know how to help the suffering and fighting being that is going forward and rising up to God.

Love is only liberating when a person sees a son of God in the person who is suffering, defeating, and being purified by his suffering. Every one of us is a child of God, wandering on earth in the image of a human creature. This created humanity gives every one of us that manner of life on earth—with all its imperfections, difficulties, and contradictions—that is unchangeably and unmistakably inherent in each of us. For this reason, we must calmly, properly, and patiently accept all subsequent pain and suffering, "carrying our cross" and learning how to constructively overcome what has been given to us. We should not be overly horrified at the sight of a suffering creature. It does not befit us to flee pain and grief at any cost. We must perceive the necessity of suffering, see its higher spiritual advantage and spiritually strengthening power, and grasp its universal purpose once and for all.

In separation (or even withdrawal) from God, the human creature must suffer. This suffering calls and leads him to God. This is why suffering is given in the first place; therein lies its meaning, such is its higher purpose. The plants and animals are subjected to this basic universal suffering in its weakest potency, and are thus unable to transform it into battle and enlightenment. But man has a higher calling: he must accept his given suffering as something "sent" to him, like a call for purification, like a willing personal battle for the sake of a fruitful enlightenment of his person.

The child of God suffers on earth because this suffering raises him up toward God: in battle and in its defeat he seeks for his holy and original native land. The torment of a creature is terrible if it neither comprehends the higher purpose of his suffering nor discovers its ascending path: he sees only pointless agony in it. But if the creature finds both purpose and path, and if this higher purpose of suffering is then realized and materialized, he should consequently be neither horrified nor reproachful; his sentimental compassion is not the final word in his secular wisdom. In this way suffering is comprehended and justified; we must accept it as a call and a blessing.

Then the great and fruitful mystery of the world will be revealed to us, and we will be able to perceive it with our heart, our gaze, and our reasoning. Our soul will be filled with the world's sorrow, yet this sorrow will truly raise us up into the heavens, nearer to God.

God is the first and highest source of living love. This is why He surely suffers at the sight of His created living creature who sighs and groans in expectation. He suffers primarily not in the world, but *for the world*, for the sighs and groans of His creatures rise up to His throne. But then He comes down to the world and takes on the image of a creature, flesh and blood, breath and pain. He takes part in the life of the world and suffers as a member of the world, together with the suffering creatures. He takes upon Himself the yoke of mankind in order to reveal and give to man the divine art of suffering, which is liberating, redeeming, and spiritually fruitful. God becomes man in order to deliver the prodigal and the blind man from the fatality of pointless suffering; God becomes man in order to raise men up to God.

A new path is revealed to man: he must see it, freely acknowledge it, and willingly choose it. Then he defeats the suffering of the world and transforms it into an opportunity, a starting point, a source of constructive purification and enlightenment. At first he learns to do this within himself, on his own person; later, he tries to teach it to other people. Then he comprehends the meaning of suffering in the world and rises higher toward an understanding of the world's true, fruitful sorrow. He sees how human creatures suffer and struggle. He sees that God takes upon Himself humanity's yoke and burden. And he carries the fruitful suffering of the world, together with humankind, and so follows in the footsteps of the Lord.

Such is the true image of the world's sorrow. Having once adopted it, man no longer prays for deliverance from misfortunes and suffering, but rather for the suffering of the world to become comprehensible, uplifting, fruitful, and enlightening—for it to be eased, for its higher purpose to be fulfilled, realized, and completed on the paths of God.

Mountains

Endless ages ago, soon after the creation of the world, when the earth felt its primordial form and boundaries for the first time, it grew sad and sorrowful. It saw itself as cast off and disgraced, torn away from the light and distanced from the heavens, evenly leveled, naked, barren, and helpless. It began to sigh and protest; it grew indignant and rose up in rebellion. This was a violent uprising, terrible and chaotic. But it came from the earth's very depths: it was sincere, and its sparks flew up to the sky: it was fiery, and its flames rose up in prayer to the Creator. And from this fire cliffs fused together, and a stream of primeval rocks poured forth. There was a great uprising of the depths, a thirst for light, a longing for the heavens, an outburst of creative will... A dream of new, ideal forms was born, a new wealth of existence—a dream of the earth drawing nearer to the heavens.

This uprising was an inclination toward God, a protesting prayer, a plea for the rejected one not to be turned away...

And the Lord, in His eternal goodness, saw these sighs and heard this plea of protest. The great uprising of the depths found a place in His good will, for while inert passivity and servile submission are never pleasing to Him, any sincere impulse or prayerful protest, such as the prayer of a yearning being, is accepted by the heavens. Thus, the Lord blessed this uprising of the earth and did not allow it to decay into nothingness, but ordered it instead to be preserved forever—to rise up to the heavens in silent prayer, to awaken with the graceful dawn, and to blissfully bloom in the last rays of the retreating sun. And God commanded man to contemplate this mysterious record of the past and come to understand its sacred meaning.

Having contemplated it, we have since given it the name *mountains*.

When I see snow-covered mountains rising up in the distance toward the clouds, my heart trembles with unexpected joy. Ancient and silenced memories awaken within me, as if I had already contemplated these images at some time past, and thus have always longed for them, as if the most wonderful and sacred promises were being fulfilled. I stand awed and overwhelmed, and do not know if I should believe this sight, so light, so bold is this sweep to the skies. How gentle, how illusory are the outlines. And how powerful are the masses of earth hidden within them. I see the earth rising up toward the heavens, I see the heavens embracing it, I see how the earth becomes lost in the heavens as they merge together—can it be that the earth itself becomes part of the heavens? Is this not a dream? Or is perhaps this vision a true reality, while the flat existence of every day is merely a weighty dream? Where did this blessed trepidation come from, this feeling of approaching my native land? It is as if this splendor shining down from afar, this promised future, has emerged from my intimate past, from my existence before the creation of time... Is my soul perhaps so "ancient of days" that I truly was present at the forming of the worlds? Or do these distant mountains perhaps recount to me what I was, what I am, what I will be—what splendor awaits me in the future?

Gentle visions, prophetic images, divine dreams… But now the sight has vanished. The airy specters have been veiled by earthly mist and heavenly clouds. Only the heart whispers to me of the possible existence of the impossible.

Later, the mountains allow me to come among them: they draw me up, calmly and serenely letting me tread upon them and scale their steep peaks. Their calmness is passed on to me, and I climb ever higher. My ascent is slow; I must not and should not hurry, for much time is needed to overcome the high altitude, to become accustomed to it so that my head stops spinning from this sleepy mountain rebellion, so that my breathing does not stop from this prayer of nature… I am already tired, but I do not want to and cannot think about my fatigue. A mysterious power calls me to the top. I am suddenly bent on going higher, higher, ever higher, as if a mighty and precipitate heave upward has taken hold of me and I am powerless to resist. Only after having exhausted all my efforts would it be possible to stop climbing and break away, but even then I would feel in my soul that I had fallen disgracefully short in a great deed. No, that would be impossible; I must keep going to the end, in order to experience the meaning and destiny of that ancient uprising for myself, to learn the restless prayer of the mountains…

Every minute brings changes to my surroundings: new precipices, unseen depths, ascending heights. Every turn reveals something unexpected. Every precipice speaks of terrible events of the past and of the possibilities of new shapes and forms. The wildest things are beautiful. The most terrible things are all in the past. This is what the earth dreamed of in its pre-eternal days, the wealth of new possibilities and new forms that it imagined then. My soul is seized with joy because it has been allowed to see and experience this ancient mystery of existence.

And then there is the air that I am breathing: at first it is aromatic and fragrant, like flowers; then thin and resinous; and finally piercingly cold, icy and burning. There below, where we dwell, the air is thick and dusty, viscous and sticky; we grow accustomed to it and never notice what we are breathing and swallowing. But here it flows down from above like water from an icy spring, like a gift from heaven, like a divine blessing. It seems severe and sharp, and one may think that there is not enough of it, that one needs more. But one must overcome this feeling and get used to it. He must remember that man is not accustomed to being close to heaven, that he is experiencing a battle, the fate of the primeval world that yearned for mountainous purity and a greater nearness to God. And nearness to God requires other abilities and new efforts from us sinful creatures...

* * *

And so at last the climb has come to an end. I am at the top, in the austere confinement of the mountains. Everything has vanished: the fragrance of flowers and giant firs, the herds of animals, the cottages. In the severe calm, I am being observed by that ancient Chaos. The bare, grayish-yellow cliffs stand in majestic silence. The plunging glaciers lie in heavy slumber, sprinkled with black rocks like dust. The overwhelming silence all around seizes my soul; I can hear the beating of my own heart and the ringing beginning in my ears...

Yes, everything that is great in the world lives in silence. And speaks with silence. If I close my eyes, I feel surrounded by utter emptiness, a total absence of being. But if I open them, I am amazed by the complete noiselessness of this plenty, these rocky masses, these imposing blocks of stone. The mountains do not like noise: they seem to have withdrawn into themselves, into their own sacred life, harboring within themselves thoughts that have been maturing for ages long past. Only landslides and avalanches, unable to endure this silent majesty, throw themselves down with a thunder and a crash; and the bubbling and boiling streams of water, slipping down into the valley, give away the secret thoughts of the mountainous heights. But the mountains themselves exclaim only with their utmost silence, only with the incomplete completeness of their design, only with the symbiosis of their outlines and their magnitude.

Silent beauty, severe goodness, humble grandeur; all of this combined together is like an eternal hymn. It is a kingdom of soundless symphonies.

* * *

One stands and listens to this soundlessness. And one learns to preserve a chaste silence in the higher spheres of life. He learns to observe his own dignity, laying claim to nothing, and he understands that true greatness is clothed in humility. No noise is necessary in the battle for the heavens, in the ascent to God; all that is necessary is for one's life to become a quiet prayer, and then it will rise up in praises and bright gratitude.

* * *

In ancient days long past, the earth sorrowed over its fate and protested to God in a great uprising. And it remained forever in this disarray. It froze in its rebellion. Its rebellion became a prayer, and its prayer was artistic chaos. And this chaos submitted to the word of God, its uprising was transformed into a hymn of thanks. The inspired surge was pacified by God's blessing, and the risen cliffs forged a friendship with the rays of the heavenly light.

The mountains rested in their silence, assuming a certain divine likeness, and through their exhortation and transfiguration revealing to mankind their mysterious purpose.

IV. VISITING

The Contemplative Poet

We, the contemplative poets, are certain that everything on earth and in heaven can be seen or heard by us, and that we are expected to produce descriptions and interpretations of it all—even those most subtle things that have no physical embodiment, things without sound, unseen, and sacred... We ourselves don't know why we are certain of this, or how we are able to do this, or what we must do to achieve it. No level of premeditation would be of help. There is no "method" that we can put forward for the task, for we cannot name as "method" our selfless dreaming, our "immersion" into contemplation, our focused "absent-mindedness," or our forgetfulness of the life surrounding us. We know as well as others that a reverie is a reverie and a dream is a dream, that fantasy can separate itself from reality, and that a poet is a poor judge in quotidian affair, for too often, in the words of the wise Heraclitus, "Present he is absent..."

"Reverie," "dream," "fantasy"... are all these things really so weak and insignificant? Can it be that the contemplative dreamer is truly nothing more than a composer, as they said in the time of Gogol? Is it true that his musings are worth nothing? Or perhaps it is the other way around: perhaps it is the contemplative poet, this daydreaming *dreamer*, who is really clairvoyant and a master in matters of true living? I do not speak, of course, of our nightly dreams, in

113

which we invariably see ourselves only in the various likenesses of others; in which we surprise and shock ourselves, seducing our own selves with different passions... No, I speak of the *visions of the contemplative poet.* That is entirely different.

We can all agree that the nature of creation, its mysterious essence (or, as they say, its "world soul") remains sacred and is not revealed lightly, let alone exhaustively. We, the poet-dreamers, decidedly do not know how other people can learn even a little about it; it is very possible that they truly know nothing about it, which sometimes they themselves openly admit. As far as we are concerned, we are inclined to acknowledge that the world has buried itself in a certain mysterious sleep. It has withdrawn into itself, sinking into its own unique depth and hiding its true essence from passing glances—and as for us we follow it, we try to overtake it, as it follows its own paths, and to perceive its *living essence.*

When a poet surrenders himself to the act of creation, he is not asleep. But in order to capture the world's mystery that has thus far eluded him, he follows its example and "falls asleep." His sober and helpless daily condition also falls asleep inside of him, along with his nearsighted perceptions and apparently "intelligent" rational thinking. This limited, dim-sighted self sinks into a slumber, dissolves into a certain spiritual twilight, and eliminates itself as a cognitive body. By doing so the poet makes way for a new spiritual contemplation, one which seems "sleepy" but in reality is inspired and profound. Then new and winged powers awaken in his soul, and new expanses are revealed to it. The floor and ceiling seem to open wide; they crumple up and disappear. The air, like the wind blowing down from the mountains, becomes transparent: the distant seems near, the invisible becomes visible, and the eye begins to see primeval beauty and depths. So the poet sees the stars in the bright sky of day, as if he was looking out of a deep well; so he hears mysterious voices of the world in the darkness of night and draws near to the most intimate powers of the world's core. As Pushkin wrote, the inspired poet heeds "the spheres revolving, chiming, the angels in their soaring sweep, the monsters moving in the deep, the green vine in the valley climbing...."[22] He enters into a different world, or quite possibly the new world enters into him and fills his being. He remains in this world; he experiences it first-hand, contemplates it, hears it, lives in its mysterious essence. He loses himself in the tapestry of this world, in its sacred, intrinsic, primeval nature of being. He "falls asleep" and "sleeps" together with the world, and sees its dreams: he contemplates the world's artistically fruitful, sacred Idea—the Divine Idea of Creation.

He lives in the world's soul, which governs all things and creatures, and he takes part in its creative act...

From an outside perspective, in ordinary, sober words, this is a "dream come to life," "a poet's dream," "a flight of fancy," perhaps even "nonsense." But in reality, this is not a dream but rather an awakening: the poet awakens for the sake of the internal and real things in life, and before him is revealed the living essence of existence.

And what he "hears" and "sees" is something completely different from what we perceive with our ordinary senses. The sun sings to him a majestic hymn; the stars carry signs and prophecies to him; he sees how the mountains pray; he hears how the brook dreams; the sea calls to him and promises him a life in eternity; the quiet, pure snow brings him wonderful consolation. The entire universe is full of slumbering love and quiet singing. The flowers guard their thoughts and humors. The birds know much that is unknown, and utter prophesies. Proud thoughts mature in the trees and the rainfall. And no one would believe the poet if he tried to tell what the wind imparted to him...

---

[22] A.S. Pushkin. Trans. Baring, Maurice, et al. *The Poems, Prose, and Plays of Alexander Pushkin* (New York: The Modern Library, Random House, Inc.) pg. 62.

While the poet drowns in this dreaming wakefulness, he cannot "create," "compose," or produce new images or forms. But this condition cannot and must not carry on overly long, or the poet may return no more to this life. It ceases and vanishes, and he returns to his daily surroundings once more. He usually returns a little dazed, weary, and helpless, but also enriched and happy. He brings back an entire treasure trove, which he can never adequately describe or formulate. Moreover, there may be much that he has lost along the way, forgotten, or never found in the first place… And that is why anything he is able to preserve and bring back with him will always seem somewhat impoverished, depleted, or perhaps even distorted. Sometimes he feels like the prince in the story who, after losing all his riches, sees only shattered fragments before him and futilely tries to count them.

And yet, and yet—he has *communed with the innermost nature of the world* and perceived its sacred essence. And everything he has accumulated and treasured wants to find true expression, profound interpretation, a beautiful manifestation, an aesthetic formulation.

It is better not to ask us how we find our way to this interpretation and this formulation. Who has the strength necessary to articulate Divine Ideas? Who can find the proper and exact expressions for them? The poet ponders this in humble helplessness; he is seized with an awareness of his inadequacy, filled with shame-faced confusion. Only the strength of that internal charge, only an inspired rising of those treasured riches to the surface, compels him to approach the matter at hand.

One person may express what he has seen in sound and song; another, through drawing. A third searches for artistically precise words. Some make models, and build; still others attempt to find the right physical movements in dance. But everything they create—these contemplating poets—comes not *from* them, but *through* them. Everything they produce is *bigger* than they; for they are merely serving as instruments, as voices for the mysterious core of the world.

And he who truly hears their song trembles inside his heart and rejoices in spirit. Little by little a new feeling forms—a new certainty that he has reached out to another world: "No, this is not a poet's fantasy. This is as *ancient* as the world...and at the same time, it is as *new* and young as the current day... What I perceived was as real as the bread of life and as precious as a revelation. I have touched upon a sacred truth of the world and found happiness."

Meanwhile, they who are not found worthy to hear the voice of the contemplating poet merely shrug their shoulders and walk away; they don't like it, they call us "storytellers" and "daydreamers" and chide us for our confidence and pretentiousness. Then we become dismayed and grow silent, retreating into our corners in confusion because we cannot "prove" anything. We can only "show," for to start an argument about our visions of another world would be both impermissible and improper...

Fire

I can sit for hours in front of the fireplace and watch the fire. A wonderful quiet descends upon my soul, and I seem to see extraordinary distances and depths. The light joyfully dances about. The shadows capriciously and whimsically settle down. The warmth gently issues forth its breath. And it seems to me that the forgotten desires of my ancestors awaken in my soul; magnificent images stand before me. I begin to understand ancient laws and eternal truths; I withdraw into the past and lose all sense of time. Joy and sadness battle within my heart, and somewhere, in the final depths, a poignant longing for my lost but holy native land is awakened. Then I feel that I know much more than I previously assumed; that I am being shown the very essence of creation; that I am touching the tip of the raiment of God...

* * *

But first we must bring the fire to life: "Come, mysterious power, visit and enlighten my dark hearth, and accept under your authority the wood that awaits you." And so that first bluish tongue of fire flames up, carefully, timidly, as if it were glancing around to make sure that it was indeed summoned—can it be assured that its meal has been prepared? … And then, answering the call and growing in trust, the flame all the more willingly, with increasing enthusiasm, comes to life, rejoices in the reverential summons and grows in the welcoming atmosphere. It grasps the logs with long tongues of flame, caressing them and taking them away, and is transformed into an unrestricted fire; the logs answer with gentle crackling and quiet whispers, both accepting and not accepting the invitation to the fire's game, and gradually heating up from its scorching breath. Then a general celebration begins with light and joy, sparkling and snapping, playing and falling down, the smoldering of the coals, and the streaming of the smoke. And the warmth, blessed, permeating, while I sit and watch, chained to my seat, contemplating this wonderful element and seeing through it the lives of men and the flow of creation. And it seems to me that no longer does time have any hold over me.

*   *   *

Our distant ancestors sat by the fireside in just this way, looking into the fire and musing over their brutal lives with all their dangers, anticipating new invasions of enemies and preparing to fight them off. For Russia's entire history has passed by in wars, and always the Russian soul has been compelled to be a ready victim. The very thing that man contemplates for a long, uninterrupted time, giving himself over to it and fully experiencing it, becomes his talent, his prototype, and his source of strength and inspiration. The human soul quietly identifies with its favorite symbol. And so, by contemplating fire, the souls of our ancestors became *fire-like*: living, light, intense, bright, shining, and strong. There is a reason why the

East created a religion of "fire-worshippers;" they saw in the flame a symbol of Divinity, granting *purification and clarity...*

But fire also taught our ancestors freedom and unity. A person's individual abode, his own home, his untouchable, free dwelling, is found wherever a fire is alive in the hearth. His hut may be small and his domestic rule modest, but in its confines he desires to be a free master and is entitled to that right. The fireside has always been the first sacred haven of *freedom and independence* for all nations. The entire family gathered around the fireplace and felt its unity; people talked to each other of their cares and their woes, their successes and their joys; they sought each other's advice concerning their needs and dangers. They lit the lamp before the icon and read the Sacred Scripture. Here they told stories and tales. And when the fire grew low, slight spectral shadows slid along the walls, fact and fiction became one, and the world of fantasy visited the sober and severe lives of the people...

What a joy to find myself again in this first of the schools of life, to surrender myself to the contemplation of this ancient element and once again perceive the experience, trials, and wisdom of my ancestors!

* * *

How airy, how light is the existence of this mysterious force! A flame, like wind, is the lightest and most mobile thing in the world. Its life is an eternal vigil, an eternal dispersion, and eternal absorption. Where the flame spurts up, there it confirms its authority and celebrates its victory. This is why it is a symbol of *joyful conquest,* effortless triumph, and victorious dance.

Could it be otherwise? Fire is the greatest force in the world. It is the source of life and the destiny of the universe—the living breath of God. It illuminates and shows the way: thus there is no clarity without fire, no revelation. Warmth and heat comes from it: this is why neither life nor love is possible without fire. It carries purification and calls us to new ways of life: he who thirsts for purity must prepare himself in spirit for fiery cleansing, and he who seeks beautiful forms must himself burn with an internal flame. Fire has the power to transform and destroy: this is why every living being is drawn to fire, and fears it.

*   *   *

Indeed, all creatures are drawn to fire—but they are also frightened when it reaches its full potential and unfolds its magnificence. How terrible it would be if fire were completely extinguished in the world, and darkness and cold were to be enthroned forever! What fear would seize the universe if flames were to engulf and completely incinerate every living thing.

But the world was created in good order. Fire's gifts were harmoniously and wisely distributed among creation. Everything partakes of it in relation to its strengths and abilities, accepting only as much of its light, intensity, and might as it can bear. And everything that takes anything from fire accepts a *divine spark*, in order to worthily answer the Creator Himself and His wonderful world out of the depths of its being.

This is where the mysterious glint emitted by precious stone comes from—that blinding ray in the diamond, that soft and velvety fire of the ruby, that flame in the yellow topaz, that sparkle in emeralds and aquamarines, that deep and hidden fire of the garnet and chrysoberyl...

As for plants, the flower, with its innocently luminescent face, was given the ability to recreate the features of the world's luminary and turn directly to it for warmth and light.

In animals, the light is focused in the eyes, with their unbridled, fierce, and therefore terrible glimmer.

But with man, a thinking and contemplating being, the light in the eye transcends that animalistic ferocity; it radiates spiritually in dealing with the world and prayerfully in turning toward the Creator.

And so it is with everything—where the fire shines, there it demands a response, and it takes pleasure in that responding ray with its own light…

* * *

This meeting of two fires—the world's fire and the individual fire—materializes most completely in man. For in man, fire becomes a *flaming spirit*, and its gifts and abilities appear in their highest and most surpassing potency. For the external, material fire was only brought to life by the breath of God as a living image of the Spirit Itself. Even the most naïve and primitive person will foresee and foreshadow this higher purpose of fire. That is why our distant ancestors, the naively wise first men, prayed to the earthly fire as to the living symbol of the Lord, venerating within it the pure breath of the Creator and celebrating its manifestation as an early revelation of God. They bowed down to the fire, but acknowledged the Spirit of God. This symbolic veneration is as ancient as the human race, and even now it continues to live inside each of us. So Heraclitus of Greece, the prophet of flame, light, and intellect, knew what he was saying when he extolled in the face of Fire a divine primary element, and when he insisted that Flame is Intellect, and Intellect is Fire…

What would become of us if we were deprived of the spiritual gifts of this, our homeland? What would we be without the heat in our hearts, without the fire in our prayer, without the illuminating clarity of cognition, without the flaming intensity of our will and our deeds, without the commanding, inspired power in our eyes? But does this not mean that all of our better assets—the most noble, most wonderful, most powerful things within us—originated in fire?

* * *

We Christians also know this great religious symbol, for by it our thoughts and feelings live. This is why we call Christ the Savior "the true Light" (John 1:9) and are baptized "in the Holy

Spirit and in fire" (Matthew 3:11; Luke 3:16). We call ourselves "sons of Light" (John 12:36) and await the Holy Spirit in the form of "tongues of fire." (Acts 2:3). And when we read the words, "I am come to send fire on the earth; and what will I, if it be already kindled?" (Luke 12:49), then fire and light descend upon our hearts, and we know of whose spirit we are.

*   *   *

But the fire is going out in my fireplace. It is dying and fading away, and I must part with it. "Go to your rest, noble and pure flame, and bless you for everything, for your light, for your warmth, and your consolation..."

By the Seaside

I dreamt for a long time of escaping the stifling city. For too long I had been languishing in that oppressive, deafening street life, in that city lifestyle full of woe and dirt, where everything weighed heavily upon me, exhausted me, and wounded my heart at every step. I longed to go there, to that watery sweep, where all boundaries are washed away and where the distance unfolds its blessed expanse... How I dreamed of the sea!

And finally it happened. One time, long ago, I experienced this joy for the first time in my life.

*   *   *

That of which I could only dream stood before me like a living vision. That distant, retreating, vanishing expanse reveals itself so quietly, gives of itself so lightly, beckons so tenderly. Your gaze clings to it, searches for its limit without finding it; you joyfully sense that even there, farther than your eye can tell, there is no limit to the expanse. Here there are no boundaries, for isn't every boundary prohibiting and disillusioning? Here there are no walls, for isn't every

wall are an injury and a threat? … Oh, how accustomed we have
become to sitting in cages! How bound we are, how depressed and
frightened in our lives! How limited is that which we can do, how
little we see, how cut off our horizons, how poor our lives! We are
deprived of so much—and we don't even notice it!

But here…here it is a celebration of expansiveness, here
governs the Limitless, here the air breathes, here dwell endless
possibilities. I drink my fill of this air, swallowing it whole. My heart
blossoms, swells with bliss, and rejoices in the flow of this permissive,
beckoning love. It is as if the world wants to impart to me something
great and good about acceptance, forgiveness, and conciliation…

*　*　*

And only later, having taken my fill of the vastness, do I
remember that I had noticed an enormous, quiet, yet moving field
of water. Calmly, powerfully, the sea rolls away its cresting waves—
where? It is dark blue, thoughtful, submerged in its own and the
heavens' thoughts. It seems languid and apparently weary, but at the
same time it is evidently playful and light, without any knowledge
of weight or awareness of its labor. To look at, it is an abundant,
countless multitude, but in reality it is a single, breathing being. It
is strange as well as welcoming, complex as well as simple. Its very
majesty lies in its reigning silence; its very essence lies in its radiating
humility and goodness. This is given to everyone, to me also, and for
me… Why for me? Oh, it is an undeserved grace! Oh, it is a mercy
unsought!

A quiet sorrow rises up in my heart—a reproach? repentance?
Why did I never "have the time?" Why am I experiencing this joy
for the first time? My God, how poor my life has been until now!
How much have I missed! How much wealth have I done without!
I see, I understand: this body of good could have lived another
eternity without me. And yet it seems to have been waiting for me,
preparing its gifts for me, ready to accept me and gladden me. Right

now it forgives me—both my long absence and my late arrival...
Everything will be presented to me, revealed to me, given to me, if
only I open my heart, listen, and contemplate it...

*   *   *

What a strange feeling seizes a person at the very edge of
water! The splashing waves seem to say, "Come up to this point and
no further," but this only awakens in my soul the need, the insistent
desire, to overstep that boundary and go farther than the indicated
point. The sea beckons and teases, but does not allow entry. No, of
course it allows and even invites entry, yet as soon as the gentle
moisture parts, it takes hold of me and drenches me... You who are
timid in nature should beware: here you will not escape or save
yourself, you will not emerge dry; you run for a brief time, splashing
about, and then it is over, you are caught... And suddenly the
timidity is gone. What frugal contact, what a welcoming meeting,
what loving treatment. It is intoxicating and delightful, calming
and invigorating... It is the only pleasure of its kind. But now the
boundary has been crossed, the deed done—and you want to do
it again and again! To reexamine that initial feeling, to repeat that
affectionate reception... Moreover, you want to surrender yourself
to this wonderful element, to touch it, stroke it; to caress, animate,
tease, splash, swim, dive, swallow, and disappear in it—to enjoy it to
the fullest. The entire time you want to experience its being and its
greeting, to accept its love and give it yours... You do this until you
achieve a total unity, a complete intimacy, until a bright friendship
develops from your blessed game...

*   *   *

I get dressed and lie down, exhausted, on the edge of the
shore in the shadow of an old pine, and listen to the voice of the sea.
It seems to me that it wants to soothe me, ease my excitement, maybe
even lull me to sleep, so that I may rest from this unwonted joy—

from this profound expanse that revealed and prepared my heart, and from this affectionate game that filled and intoxicated it. I close my eyes and concentrate. A multitude of streaming and babbling voices whispers to me of one thing. At first I hear what seem like quiet reproaches, but they melt away in the breath of gentle forgiveness. With them disappears the last shadow of sadness, and the sorrow in my heart is healed. After that come hopes and promises; they emerge out of some ancient, deep, forgotten depths and bring me tales of life in paradise, and of its marvelous innocence...

My heart becomes filled with a sweet, inexplicable joy—light, beckoning, not committing me to anything. I want to listen forever, only giving thanks and never wishing for anything more. Minute after minute, the quiet murmur of a wave creeps up; it gurgles and pleasantly whispers, as if understanding me and watching over my repose; it foams and grows still, as if casting a spell on me; it gently boils and rustles and breathes over me, as if wanting to evoke unspoken visions in my heart—to cover me with blessed dreams and to assure me, verifying that these are no dreams, but prophecies and promises.

To this day I still do not know if I was asleep or awake, lulled by the whisper of the waves. Perhaps I awoke in my dream to a new life. That which once was vanished and never appeared again. I felt that the good and eternal bosom of the world had accepted me into its quiet love and revealed to me its purest of expanses... I was allowed to look into this hidden womb of existence, come into contact with those places where we once lived in trusting innocence, where to this day God's forgiveness and love await us... And from that point, I have carried in my heart an unshakable certainty that all of man's suffering is meaningful and necessary, that he must suffer his way to a free and holistic return to God—that loving forgiveness, gracious protection, a healing return to innocence, and the wisdom of blessed contemplation await us all...

* * *

When I came to, the sun was setting, disappearing into the sea, and I didn't know how long I had been absent. I lay on the shore under the pine, and everything I had experienced felt like a dream. Only the flow of joy held my entire being: this joy was like light, the light felt to me like love, and this love granted me healing and ecstasy. And I felt that I had entered into communion with some indefinable and inexhaustible good, for which we mortals have not yet found the right words. What I was able to express in words seemed to me merely the threshold of the sacred, only the entryway to the temple I had glimpsed...

My face was moist. Was it tears? If so, they were the tears of a healed man, tears of joy and gratitude. Or perhaps it was a greeting from my newborn-ancient primal birthplace. In that case I would like to guard this feeling for the duration of my life and pass it on to others, so that they too might experience the joy of forgiveness and renewal that I had experienced.

*　*　*

And now if I am visited by sorrow, or if I am seized by melancholy and my eyes become full of tears, then they are a new and different kind of tears, which I am unable to distinguish from the blessed moisture of my original birthplace. For I have visited divine shores, and I know surely that a heart can only bear so much pain, while there is no limit to love and forgiveness, and that any pain or grief is only a preparation for bliss, that it is only a first step toward the enlightenment of the spirit.

About Suffering

The minute we feel that we are suffering, physically or spiritually, we must immediately remember that we do not suffer alone—and that every suffering, without exception, has some higher purpose. We will immediately feel relief.

We do not suffer alone because the whole world suffers around us. We only need to open our heart and look closely, and we will see that we are one with the suffering of the universe. *Everything* suffers and experiences pain—some suffer in soundless silence, hiding their pain, silencing their agony, overcoming their suffering within themselves, while some suffer with open expression, which no one or nothing can abate... Languishing in love, sighing from discontent, lamenting pleasure itself, struggling in lengthened battle, sadness, and anguish: all earthly creatures live in suffering, beginning with their first helpless act—the birth from the mother's womb—and ending with their last earthly act—their mysterious departure "to rest." So mankind suffers along with the rest of creation as a microorganism of the world, as a child of nature. We cannot escape suffering; it is our fate, and we must come to terms with it. It is natural to wish that our suffering be minimal. But we must learn to suffer *honorably* and *spiritually*. This is the great mystery of life; this is the art of our earthly existence.

Our suffering arises from a way of life that is unique to us as people, one that has been given to us once and for all and which we cannot change. The minute we develop self-awareness, we are convinced of our independence and helplessness. Man is a creature designed for "an existence of self," for self-reliance and self-sustainment; at the same time, he serves all of nature as if passively, or walking through a revolving door. On the one hand, nature looks after him like its own child: it cultivates him, builds him and is present in him, taking pleasure in him like something unique and unparalleled; on the other hand, it sows in him such contrasts, unfurls in him such chaos, and surrenders him to such diseases that it would seem as if it knew neither expediency nor mercy. Thus, I am designed and predestined to act independently, but woe to me if I trust in my total independence or try to surrender myself to it completely! I am a liberated spirit, but this liberated spirit remains subjugated to all of life's needs and limited by all the impossibilities of existence for the duration of its life. A certain generalizing power of consciousness lives inside me, taking hold of worlds and opening wide immense spiritual horizons for me, but this power is confined within the walls of its solitary body for its entire life; it weakens from hunger, faints away from exhaustion, runs dry from lack of sleep. I am isolated from other people, immured in my soul and body, and doomed to lead a solitary life, for I can neither allow anyone else inside nor accommodate anyone within my limits. And at the same time other people torment my soul and can tear apart my body as if I were their toy or slave... This is what I am, and such are we all, every one of us individually—flowers that live for but a day, blossoming only to suffer, momentary and unprotected bursts of universal flame...

> *"Your life, O mortals, is such a fragile gift of the gods:*
> *you blossom for a moment, living giants...."*
> A.D. Illichevskii

Do any of us truly "blossom?" We, the eternal "patients" of nature, submissive recipients of the world's emanations, most sensitive of organs surpassing nature? We are partly regal and partly enslaved, with something from God and something from the worm;[23] we are so much and yet so little, free and bound, the world's purpose and the victims of the universe. Enslaved angels, creatures of divine artistry, given away as food to bacteria and waiting to become burial ashes...

That is why suffering comes upon us so often and so easily; and that is why we must come to terms with it. The more refined a person is, the more sensitive his heart, the more responsive his conscience, the stronger his artistic imagination, the more impressionable his powers of observation, the more profound his soul—the more he is doomed to suffer, the more often he will experience pain, sorrow, and bitterness in life. But we often forget about this; we don't think about our common fate and completely fail to understand that

---

[23] G.P. Derzhavin. "Ode to God."

the best people suffer the most... And when we ourselves experience a downpour of deprivations, torments, afflictions, and desperation—when, as now, the entire world is submerged in sadness and shudders with every articulation, sighing, lamenting, and calling out for help—we become frightened, draw back in wonder, and protest, considering it all "unusual," "undeserved," or "pointless."

We must come to the gradual realization that every person is subject to the law of earthly creatures. At first we get an uneasy sense that there is much more suffering on earth than we imagined in our childish expectations. This sensation worries us; we try to reexamine it and gradually, by indescribable ways, by an almost shapeless intuition, we become convinced that we have truly discovered the *law of existence*, a universal way of life governing all earthly creatures, which states that there is no existence without suffering, that every earthly creature by his very nature is designed to suffer and doomed to mourn. Moreover, a man with a gentle heart knows more than this: he also knows that not only do we suffer together, in conjunction with one another, but all of us contribute to each other's torment—whether by accident or by design, through carelessness or through cruelty; passionately, coldly, or in a fatal crossing of life paths... And perhaps it was Dostoevsky himself, that master of the tortured heart, who was destined to shed light on this earthly tragedy...

Such is life; such is reality. And could it have been otherwise? And would we be correct if we began to desire and demand another way?

Let us imagine for a moment another, inverted portrayal of the world. Let us imagine that earth's creatures have been freed from all suffering, completely and forever; that some mighty voice said to them: "Creatures, do what you will. You are set free of suffering. From now on, you will not know dissatisfaction. No bodily pain will strike you. Neither sorrow, nor anguish, nor spiritual fragmentation will come to you. No spiritual anxiety will come near your soul. From this point on, you are sentenced to eternal and absolute contentment. Go and live." Then a new, unprecedented age would begin in the history of mankind…

Let us imagine that man has forever lost the gift of suffering. Nothing threatens him with dissatisfaction; hunger and thirst, those primary sources of effort and suffering, have ceased altogether, as well as dissatisfaction with oneself, with other people and the world. The sense of imperfection has vanished forever, and with it the desire for perfection. Every possible trace of deprivation, which before had urged man forward, has fallen away. Bodily pain, which warns man of impending danger to his health and awakens his adaptability, resourcefulness, and inquisitiveness, has been taken away. Every aberration of nature is now protected and goes unpunished. Any ugliness and abomination in life are of no concern to the new man. Moral indignation, previously arising from contact with ill will, has disappeared. Painful reproaches of the conscience have been forever silenced. Spiritual thirst, which before led people to the desert, to great asceticism, has ceased for good. Everyone is content with everything; everyone likes everything; everyone indulges in everything without measure or choice. Everyone lives in promiscuous, primitive hedonism—yet this hedonism is neither passionate (for passion is tormenting), nor intense (for intensity is possible only where strengths are not wasted), but rather accumulated due to abstinence.

How can I describe the terrible, devastating consequences that would fall upon mankind once it has been doomed to absolute contentment?

The world would see the rise of a new, despicable breed of "anthropoids"—a breed of indiscriminating hedonists surviving on the very lowest of spiritual levels. These would be non-repentant, lazy idlers; irresponsible loafers with no interests, no temperament, no fire, no drive, no flight; lovers of no one and nothing—for love is first of all a sense of deprivation and hunger. They would be amoral, tasteless idiots, self-satisfied fools, lecherous *Lemures*.[24] Imagine their undifferentiated, expressionless faces, those flat, low foreheads, those dead, shallow gazers that used to be eyes, those pointlessly smacking mouths... Do you hear their inarticulate speech, that indifferent mumbling of eternal satiety, that hapless laughter of idiots? It is frightening to think of their lost spirituality, their dumb turpitude, the denigration of these half-men who exclude nothing, who have been cursed by God and doomed never to deal with suffering...

And when you imagine this scene, you see and feel what the *gift of suffering* gives to us; and you want to beg all heavenly and earthly doctors, for God's sake, to never deprive people of this gift. For without suffering, a quick and tragic end would come to us all—to our dignity, our spirit, and our culture.

This is what it gives to us. With what depth do the eyes of a suffering man shine! It is as if the walls which enclose his spirit have parted, and the mists which shroud his sacred nature have been cleared. How meaningful, how refined and noble are the features on the face of a long and honorably suffering person! And how simple, how unattractive is a smile that doesn't at least hide some suffering that has passed! What educational and purifying power is inherent in spiritually comprehended suffering! For suffering *awakens the spirit of a person*, leading him, forming and shaping him, cleansing and ennobling him... Spiritual differentiation, selection of the best, and any perfecting of self would be impossible on earth without suffering. This is where inspiration is born. Persistence, courage, composure, and strength of character are tempered through suffering. Without it there is no true love or true happiness. And he who wants to learn freedom must overcome suffering.

And yet we would like to renounce it? We would be willing to lose all this? For what?

---

[24] Lemures, or larvae: in Roman mythology, these were vengeful spirits, ghosts of the dead buried without rites, who wandered the earth at night and drove people to insanity.

Hegel once said that everything great on earth is created out of passion. We can say more and speak more deeply about suffering: we are obligated to it for *everything*, for creativity great and small. For if people did not suffer, they would not be driven to artistic contemplation, prayer, or spiritual development. Suffering is like the salt of life; the salt's strength should not be wasted. Even more so, suffering is the *driving force of life*; the foremost source of human creativity; a keen and watchful teacher of moderation; a faithful guard and wise counselor; a strict call to seek refinement and perfection; a guardian angel protecting mankind from vulgarity and demeaning of self. Wherever this angel begins to speak a reverent silence reigns, for he makes an appeal for responsibility and the purification of our lives; he speaks of error and temptation; he demands that we come to our senses and transform ourselves. He speaks of falls from grace and of disharmony, of healing, enlightenment, and the blessedness that is within our very reach...

A suffering person steps onto the path of purification, self-liberation, and a return to his native bosom, whether he knows this or not. He is drawn to the great bosom of harmony; his soul seeks a new way of life, new contemplation, new synthesis, polyphonic harmony. He searches for a path that might lead him through catharsis toward a wonderful balance, conceived specifically for him by the Creator. The sacred and creative wisdom of the world calls him to itself in order to take possession of him and heal him. The simple folk know this truth and express it with the words "a visit from God." The man who has been sent suffering must never feel that he is ill-fated or cursed, but rather "sought out," "visited," and "called upon"; he *has been allowed to suffer in order to be cleansed.* All the healings in the Gospel attest to this with great clarity.

This is the purpose of all suffering. The only thing that remains undecided is the fate of the suffering person: either he will achieve purification and harmony in his present earthly life, or these gifts will be given to him only through the loss of his earthly physical shape.

Suffering witnesses to a divergence, a dissonance, between the suffering person and God-created nature: it expresses this man's fall from nature and signifies at the same time the beginning of his return and healing. Suffering is a mysterious self-healing of a person, body and soul: he himself fights for the renewal of his life's internal order and harmony; he works on his own transformation; he seeks to "return." His deliverance has already begun, he is already on the way; he must hearken to this mysterious process, adapt to it, and contribute to it. One can say to him: "Man, assist in your own suffering to help it faithfully complete its task. For it will cease only when it has completed this task and met its goal."

For this reason we must not try to elude our suffering, to deliver ourselves from it by fleeing it, and deceiving ourselves in the process. We must stand with it face to face, heed its voice, understand and make sense of its plea, and meet it head on. This means that we must accept it as a natural and spiritually comprehended event. For it has appealed to us out of the world's own advisability: that which suffers in us is, so to speak, the very substance of the world, which yearns to creatively restore in us its life balance. And if a person obeys his suffering and meets it head on, he will soon become aware of the fact that whole stockpiles of vital strength are come to light from within him, engaging in battle in the hopes of removing the reason for his suffering.

This is why a man should not be afraid of his suffering. He must remember that the burden of his suffering (at least a third, sometimes a good half) is actually his *fear in the face of suffering.*

Neither is it good, however, for a person to do the opposite, i.e., to cause himself to suffer purposefully or willfully. Those who torment themselves, who engage in self-flagellation or castrate themselves, are wrong. They are wrong because they have been assigned a most difficult internal battle: the battle of the spirit with its passions, as well as the accompanying soulful and spiritual suffering. Yet they do not wish to undertake this battle: they turn it into a suffering of the material flesh, substitute it with bodily pain, and exchange it

for mutilation of the organs. A thermometer shows physical
temperature; one would be foolish and mistaken to breathe on the
thermometer, forcing the mercury level up, or setting it on a piece
of ice to lower the mercury level. Hunger, thirst, and love's longing,
inspiration and creation, must come on their own, enforced naturally
by the body, soul, and spirit; poisons that stimulate, depress, or
cause a state of ecstasy are false and go against nature. To make the
mistake of defying nature is to forcefully pervert it. Everything good
and true comes about by our own initiative, naturally, harmonically,
or, as Aristotle said, "δι'αὐτοῦ" (through oneself). We are designed
to live creatively and love fruitfully; to calmly, courageously, and
with wise obedience accept the suffering that draws near; and, most
of all, to constructively transform and illuminate the suffering that
has already come upon us. For suffering is not merely a payment for
healing, but a call to transformation of life and illumination of the
soul; it is a path leading to perfection, a ladder to spiritual cleansing.
A man must carry his suffering calmly and surely, for ultimately and
most profoundly, the very wellspring of the Divine suffers in us, with
us, and for us. This is the final and highest purpose of our suffering,
of which the healings in the Gospel speak.

That is why a suffering person must never become impatient,
or even less so, despondent. On the contrary, he must constructively
accept and overcome his suffering. If he is given physical pain, then
he must find the organic mistakes he is making in his life and try
to eliminate them. At the same time, he must exalt and deepen his
spiritual life to such an extent that its intensity and fire distract his
stored-up vital energy from his physical pain. We shouldn't give in to
physical pain, dwelling on it, constantly hearkening to it, or fearing
it; this would signify that we admit its victory and surrender to it,
thereby rendering ourselves mere wailing creatures. We must counter
pain of the flesh with spiritual focus, heeding not bodily torment,
but spiritual realities. And if someone should say that he doesn't have
the ability or cannot step onto that path, then let him earnestly pray
for this ability and that strength, and simply try to go down that

path. No one can do everything, or has every skill, and the skill of drawing inspiration from suffering is one of the highest. Of course, we need a certain higher power in order to conquer our infirmity, but this higher power can be achieved through prayer, earned and acquired. And every effort, every exertion in this direction will be rewarded handsomely and beyond expectation.

But if a person is given spiritual suffering, which can be much more difficult and tormenting than any physical anguish, then first of all he must not flee from it, but accept it, i.e., find the time necessary to *surrender* himself to it. He must stand face to face with his spiritual suffering and train himself to contemplate its nature and the reason for its existence. He must learn to look freely and calmly into the depth of his suffering soul with prayer in his heart, and a steady confidence in his forthcoming victory. The primary reason for his suffering will gradually be revealed to his spiritual eye, and he must then call this reason by its name, saying these words internally to himself and then uttering them before the face of God in an inner prayer of purification. In order to conquer his spiritual torment, first and foremost he must not fear it or ever despair; he must not give in to its terrors and whims, its willfulness and secret pleasures (for spiritual torment always conceals unhealthy instinctual pleasures). He must always appeal to it creatively, with the authoritative voice of the beckoning master. He must always speak to it from the person of his spirit and learn to put an end to it by commanding it, departing from it, and exerting constructive effort. He must clear its mists, deceits, and delusions, transforming its power into a joy in the divine realities in his life. This is the path that will lead him out of darkness into enlightenment and transfiguration of soul. Thus, the sacred purpose of spiritual suffering can be compared to a child slumbering in the womb of his mother and awaiting his birth, for suffering is not a curse, but a blessing; in it is hidden a certain spiritual charge, the beginning stages of new comprehensions and achievements—a wealth of sorts, fighting for its realization.

If, however, a person is in the grips of spiritual apathy, then he must purify it through prayer in order to transform it into a true and pure sorrow for the world, and thus raise the sufferer toward God. For sorrow for the world is ultimately and in the most profound sense God's own sorrow, and sorrowing together with Him is an "easy yoke" and a "light burden" (Matthew 11:30).

This is why the Apostle James wrote: "Is any among you afflicted? Let him pray" (James 5:13). For prayer is no less than the rising of the spirit to God; it is "those groanings which cannot be uttered" where "the Spirit Itself maketh intercession for us" (Romans 8:26). Prayer is a call for help, directed to Him who calls me to Himself through my suffering, and it becomes a fruitful beginning of a fruitful transformation and the enlightenment of my being.

However, none of this can be done "for me" or "instead of me," the one who suffers: all of this is my own personal matter, my effort, my ascent, my flight upward, my fruitful transformation. Another person may help me with counsel, and the Lord will always help me by giving me strength and light. But only I can complete my own purification and enlightenment. That is why freedom is required, for none of this would be possible without freedom. Freedom of contemplation, love, and prayer comprise the very essence of this fruitful mystery—the mystery of earthly suffering. And this mystery, specifically, is what lays down the faithful path that leads to true joy on earth.

About Death
(The First Letter)

My dear. You wanted to know what I think about death and immortality, and I am ready to lay out for you my understanding of it. I did not invent these ideas, but have suffered and born them over the course of many long years. And now that such a time has come when death hangs over us all, and each of us must prepare himself to depart this earthly life, I have reexamined my experiences and views

and will tell you what conclusions I have reached. In such times as
these, all of us sense and anticipate our approaching end, and for this
reason we unconsciously return in our thoughts and imagination
to the problem of death. At this a person may feel dismayed and
depressed, because he does not know what death really is, and also
because none of us can come to terms with our own death or include
its reality in our lives. Times like our current ones are usually called
"difficult" and "terrible," but in reality they are times of spiritual trial
and renewal—severe yet beneficial times when God visits us.

You see, I have always had the sense that there is something
serene, forgiving, and healing about death. And here is why.

I only need to think about this, my earthly person—in
every way imperfect, burdened through inheritance, eternally diseased,
in essence unsuccessful in the eyes of both nature and parents—and
ask, what if it were made *immortal*? Am I filled with genuine horror
at the thought? What a pitiful image: a complacent inadequacy that
is determined not to die, but to *fill all of time with itself.* An imperfection that will suffer neither correction nor extinction…an endless
flaw, an eternal blunder. It would be like a false chord that plays
forever, or a stubborn stain on the earth and sky. I see—in the shape
of my own person—this physical and spiritual mistake of nature,
destined never to die, and think how in the meantime the laws of
nature would continue on with their former inflexibility, while I will
become all the more old and probably infirm, all the more helpless,
frightening, and dimwitted—and so on and so forth, forever. What
pretension, what unhappiness! After these visions I wake up, as if I
were fast asleep, to blessed reality—to a death that certainly awaits
me… How good that it will come and establish its boundary! How
wonderful that it will put an end to my earthly disharmony! This
means that the world's mistake which bears my earthly name can be
extinguished and corrected… And death will come like a redeemer,
or a healer. It will mercifully cover me with its shelter. It will give me
forgiveness and release. It will open to me new and better possibilities.
And I will accept the freedom it gives me; emboldened by it, I will
begin my ascent to the most exalted harmonies.

And it is this anticipation, this certainty, which gives my entire life *moderation and form*. Thank God, all my earthly passionate turmoil, this endless battle with my own self, with my adversaries, and with the blind indifference of the human masses, this battle in which I exhaust myself from time to time to the point of torment and despair, will not go on forever, will not fill all the ages of God. I need not always nurse these wounds that result from the meeting of my infirmity with the unreasonable demands of this life and this world. The time will come and "separate the ox from the plough at the last furrow...."[25] The endless continuity falls away and my life receives a *measured term*: a measure of obligation, a measure in exertion, a measure of captivity, and a measure of suffering. How lovely this is! My life acquires *form*—the form of a materializing end. I know, I firmly know, that this release will come, that my liberating exodus will be revealed, and that I must prepare for it. Most importantly, I must try to make my earthly ending not a sudden break, but a *conclusion* to my whole life; all my goals, labors, and creative efforts must lead to this conclusion. It is true that I don't know how and when my death will come. But even this is a blessing, for it requires me to be ready always and for anything, to respond and to depart. One thing is certain: by taking human measures, I recognize that the end of my term is not far off, and that I cannot lose any time. I cannot put off what must be done. At the same time there is much that needs to be eliminated completely, and removed from my path. My time is limited, and no one knows to what extent. And when I look around me, I see that the immeasurable, wonderful abundance of the world, of nature, human society, and culture— all these possibilities for contemplation and joy, these occasions for spiritual perception and spiritual output, these creative callings and tasks—is inexhaustible, demanding, most difficult, and binding...

In this manner the reality of death becomes for me a finalizing and illuminating *beginning of life*, almost a summons or

---

[25] A.S. Pushkin. "Rodrig."

counsel. It is as if my oldest friend, loving and caring, would say to me: "Do you know, life is short, but there is no end to its wonderful possibilities—in love, in service, in contemplation, in creation; would it not be better to lay aside all things vulgar, pitiful, and insignificant, and choose for yourself only the best, truly the best things, which are genuinely beautiful, so as not to squander God's beauty in the world and in life?"

In a way, the idea of death opens my eyes and draws out of me a kind of insatiable hunger, a thirst for true quality, a will for divine content, the decision to select and choose correctly, without being mistaken or deceived. I slowly learn how to discern between what is truly good and wonderful before the face of God and what only seems to be good, but in reality tempts, seduces, and disillusions. And going through this trial of life, I grow more and more certain that in life there are many different types of elements, occupations, and interests that are neither worth living by nor worthy of life, while on the other hand there are some that reveal and embody life's true meaning. And in these matters of distinction and discernment, death offers me a faithful gauge and true standard.

It seems to me that all of us have already experienced, and will again experience, something similar: when death approaches (or, at the very least, its shadow is cast over us), then our life's values and elements are somehow, suddenly, reassessed almost on their own. Everything that seemed faded, meaningless, almost devoid of value in the dim light of day, during our dull and safe existence, suddenly reveals its distinction, shows its real worth, and finds its true place and proper rank. The eye of death looks starkly and sternly; not everyone in life can bear its insistent gaze. Everything vulgar immediately bares its insignificance, like a sheet of paper that upon catching fire suddenly burst into bright flames and immediately blackens, crumbles, and disintegrates into ash—so much so that in retrospect we can't believe that those ashes and dust could ever have seemed important or valuable. On the other hand, everything truly valuable, significant, and sacred becomes confirmed in the face of death and triumphantly emerges from its fiery trial, appearing in its true radiance and glory. The former is disrobed and exposed, while the latter is justified and truly sanctified. At the same time, we are never the ones responsible for bringing this about; no, this trial by fire comes from death and is caused by its approaching breath.

There are days and moments in life when a person suddenly sees death before him. These are terrible moments; these are blessed days. At these times death, like some divine emissary, judges our life. Our entire life flashes before our spiritual eyes like strokes of lightning. Everything that was true and good, everything truly worth living by, is confirmed like a veritable reality and rises up in radiance, while on the other hand everything petty, false, and insignificant is shamed and humiliated. And then we curse all that deceit and vulgarity, declaring ourselves squanderers of strength and foolish spendthrifts. At the same time we rejoice at everything true and genuine, wondering how we could hitherto have lived in any other way. We hear in the depths of our soul how everything that had been lost grieves and begs to be restored; and we ourselves begin to wish that our former life might be considered a "rough draft," giving us the opportunity to lead our future life as the "final draft." Plans for a new, wonderful life are instantly born and oaths of loyalty to it silently uttered, while prayers to God for the granting of new deadlines and new opportunities rise up...

And when the danger of death has passed, restoring peace and quiet, we see that our entire life has been pulled apart and winnowed, and we make one of our most important life conclusions: *not everything that we live by is worthy of our life's dedication.* Only if the things and actions that constitute our lives fear neither death nor its approach, only if they can be justified and confirmed before its face, can they be considered fully worthy. Everything that is worthy of our choice and preference, of our love and service even in the hour of our death, is wonderful and proper. The things for which we can and must give up our lives are the things we must love and serve. Life is only worth that for which we will fight to the death and give up living; everything else is of little value or significance. Anything not worth dying for is not worth living for, either. For death is a touchstone, a great standard, and a terrible judge.

This is how I reflect upon death, my friend. Death is not merely gracious; not only does it deliver us from this earthly vale and relieve us of the world's excessive burden, not only does it shape our lives and require of us an artistic conclusion, but it is also a certain mysterious, God-given "measurer of all things" and of all human deeds. We need it not only as a breaker of chains and a great door to our final departure; we need it first of all *in life itself and for life itself.* Its cloudy shadow is not given to us to deprive us of light or to extinguish in our soul the readiness and taste for life. On the contrary, death nurtures in us this very taste for life, fine-tuning and refining it; it teaches us not to waste time, to want the best, to choose the single wonderful thing out of many, and to live by the divine on earth for the duration of our brief life. The shadow of death teaches us to live in light. Its breath seems to whisper to us, "Come to your senses, take control, and live as an immortal in mortality." Its approach makes our weak, near-sighted eyes clear and far-sighted. And its final arrival sets us free from the burden of being and from bodily individuation. Why should any of this cause us to curse it or deem it the beginning of evil and darkness?

I understand how death's finality and irrevocability, its mystery and inscrutability, can inspire trepidation. But the flow of life in which we ever find ourselves is equally irrevocable at every moment, equally mysterious and unfathomably complex. Every instant of our earthly journey is gone without return and, dying out, is carried away into some abyss. And this abyss of the past, as well as the approaching abyss of the future, is no less frightening than the instant of our impending death. Life is no less mysterious than death; we simply close our eyes to this truth and become accustomed to not seeing it. Yet death, seen and understood properly, is nothing more than a *unique and noble act of each person's life*. And if a person sees and understands death for what it is, it will become for him like a new friend, careful, faithful, and wise.

About Immortality
(The Second Letter)

But you also wanted to know, my friend, if I recognize the immortality of a person's soul. I would like to answer that question most directly and sincerely, without any theological scholarship.

I will tell you truthfully that the thought of a final, traceless disappearance of my spiritual persona seems to me pointless, blindly conceived, and devoid of life. I consider this "possibility" a ridiculous and inveterate impossibility, not even worthy of discussion, like expounding upon the idea of dark light, powerless strength, or non-existence in being. Some people veer toward empty and constructive thinking. They don't like to proceed from realities; they are drawn to regularity in and progression of thought; a lack of foundation does not frighten them, and they do not believe in truth. It is they who should be asked to take on concepts such as "the mortality of the living spirit." However, my inherent sense of reality shies away from that. Every person, and especially every educated researcher, must possess a certain faithful instinct—an eye that is experienced in contemplation, the intuitive perception of an object and its objective nature—in order to keep from falling prey to such temptations or wasting his time discussing empty and abstract possibilities, chasing after such phantom logic, and lapsing into lifeless, if "coherent," scholasticism. Unreal possibilities are *impossibilities*, idle fiction. And he who wants to speak of *real possibilities* is obligated to find corresponding realities and hold on to them.

This is why I would like to establish that declarations about the death of our spiritual persona should only be made by someone who is either completely devoid of spiritual experience or who does not desire to participate in it or use it as a support. Such a man, perhaps, also proceeds from an entirely sensory experience of natural science, one that has been rationally reworked and which is spiritually unconcerned, and one that he recognizes as the only acceptable and true experience. But it is also possible that such a man proceeds from a literal understanding of some philosophical or religious book in which nothing is said about this—or, more to the point, the complete opposite is written. But in all of these instances people disregard the true primary source, miss the genuine experience of the spirit as well as actual spiritual realities, and make judgments of something which is hidden from them.

That tried-and-true source, that genuine reality, must be experienced personally and independently by every one of us; we must bear it within us in order to judge it from within. If someone has never had this experience, if it is completely out of his reach, then it would hardly seem possible to give him even a rather vague idea of the spirit or its existence, while to present "proof" of it would be completely impossible. But if he has at least some feeble sense of the spirit, a "mustard seed" of this experience, a smoldering spark hidden underneath the ashes of quotidian life yet still capable of producing a flame, then it is probably possible to show him everything that matters and thus come to a mutual understanding.

What I mean by all this is the *living experience* of our non-material, non-physical *spiritual existence.*

It is frightening for us, born of earth, to think of death. It is frightening to imagine that our physical person will disintegrate and surrender to decay. It is frightening for us that our earthly conscious-ness and self-awareness—fastened to our body, tied to it, limited by it, but still enriched by it—will be extinguished. All of my "here and now" will cease. My entire earthly spiritual-physical order will be disordered. What will remain of me then? Will anything remain at all? What will become of me? Where will I go? What is this traceless, mysterious disappearance into eternal silence? The question arises,

seeks a resolution, and remains unanswered. Darkness. Abyss.
Nevermore.

There is, however, a key to this agonizing riddle, a way
to approach this terrifying mystery. More specifically, no one can
give me an answer to this question except me; only I myself can do
this, and what's more, only through my own internal experience.
In this experience I must undergo and see my own spiritual essence
and acquire for myself a clear sense of my spiritual immortality.
Until I do this, anyone else's response, however cleverly it may be
formulated, will seem unclear, unconvincing, and inconclusive to
me. No earthly language contains the appropriate words or distinct
expressions for these circumstance. And because of this I am forced
to learn independently—to master, or more precisely *artfully recreate*
within myself—the required transcendental language to the point of
understanding and wielding it. If, for example, I do not understand
Chinese, I will remain at a loss, learn nothing, understand nothing,
no matter how many living witnesses speak to me in Chinese about
Chinese events. In order to behold the transcendental, I must realize
and formulate in myself a transcendental way of life, out of which
later stems *transcendental language.* And all this must be done within
the boundaries of earthly life.

It is frightening to us, born of earth, to think of death,
because we do not know how to tear ourselves away from the earthly,
sensory-physical method of living and thinking. Being incapable
of this, we hold fast to our bodies as our salvation. We recognize
it as our most important thing, our true essence, when it is only a
God-given "door" leading to the external material world with all of
its burdensome weight and ethereal beauty. And when we realize
that this "door" refuses to serve us and crumbles into dust, when we
consider that our body will become "voiceless, breathless" flesh, then
we anxiously begin to concede that this really must be our complete
and utter end.

We cannot and should not despise, or even more, "reject"
our body; after all, it admits us into this material world, full of

intelligence and beauty; it reveals to us every miracle of God's creation, all the significance, purity, and majesty of material nature. The body is the necessary and natural instrument of our communion with God's world, our participation in it; and while we are alive, it must remain at our willing and healthy disposal. The body is not given to us in vain, for the world of nature into which it admits us is the mysterious and hidden *incarnation of the thought of God*, the living and artistic symbol of His wisdom, but so that we also might become participants of this incarnation and this symbol, its living members, its organic expression. How marvelous and how wondrous that this admission was revealed to us! But it is better that it is revealed to us for a time and then will be taken away and hidden, for we are intended for something higher, more perfect, and more exquisite.

It is therefore evident that our body enters into the earthly structure of our individual personality. But it is also evident that it does not enter into the order of our spiritual being. This we must recognize while still living. We must learn not to overestimate our body, but to assign to it the fitting place and proper rank in our existence.

Man is capable of more than sensory-physical experience. Another experience, not sensory but still objective, is also available to him. We must nurture this experience, purifying it and surrendering ourselves to it. We have been given the ability to extract ourselves from bodily sensations and sensory impressions, to withdraw our focus and contemplation inward, into the depth of the spirit and the soul's dimensions, and to liberate the integral core of our persona from the oppression and delusion of matter. Surrendering ourselves to this ability and nurturing it within us, we gradually uncover our meta-physical being and confirm it as the most important and significant one. We acquire a supersensory experience, full of supersensory content, which assures us of the existence of spiritual laws and objects. And the first thing that is revealed to us at that point is our own *spiritual identity*.

My spiritual "I" is revealed to me when I become convinced that I am a creative force, a force not material in itself but designed to govern my body as its symbol, its instrument, its raiment. This spiritual force has the power not only to serve its earthly body but to rule over it; it is able to abstract itself from it and control it; it does not consider the body the moderator of all things. This creative force lives for the sake of other values and serves other goals. It has different standards and criteria. It has completely different forms, laws of life, paths, and a different condition than other bodies, and in general all matter. These forms are spiritual independence and freedom; these laws are of spiritual dignity and responsibility; these paths lead to spiritual purification and self-perfection. And this condition is one of *immortality and sonship of God*. This force, as such, is primarily and essentially the *spark of God*, and man is designed to accept and confirm in himself this godly spark as his own genuine essence; man must give himself to this spiritual spark, lose himself in it and, in so doing, find himself again. Then he himself will become God's spark and will be able to ignite it into a true flame, becoming in the process a *burning bush of the spirit*.

Yet in reality it is not the case that a man remains dual and divided, so that God's spark burns in man by itself and he lives by its strength, its forms, and its content while his physical body smolders on its own, with all its weaknesses and needs, in all of its brute nature and mortality. No: man is predestined for unity; he is designed to be a living and creative *entirety*. My spirit—that creative spark of God—was created to pierce through my soul and burn through my body, transforming both body and soul into its instrument and symbol, cleansing them from the burden of mortality and artfully transfiguring them. We are each given our own spark, and this spark wants to burst into flame within us, to become a burning bush whose flames must take hold of our entire person and turn us into God's fire, a certain *earthly beacon* of Almighty God. And so, in the course of our life's development, the spark of God becomes

humanized and individualized, and the person confirms his existence
and is sanctified in his work. The person becomes an artistic product
of God, a personal bearer of His Light, an individual hieroglyph of
the Spirit of God. Even one who comes into passing contact with
this mystery of union, this divine art in the human soul, will
immediately understand and accept these words of St. Seraphim of
Sarov: "God cares for each of us as if we were His only child."

And when suddenly I hear that this incarnate spark of
God, this artistic creation of His Spirit, in which God's grace and
man's own freedom have combined and joined in an artful mystery,
is capable of dying, falling apart, vanishing into nothingness,
emptiness, and death...must I treat this vacuous fabrication of the
blind seriously and accept it at face value? These spiritually blind
people regard as sacrosanct the law of the preservation of earthly
matter and physical energy: it is an authority which they do not
doubt. And for that very reason that the spirit is neither matter nor a
physical force, they preach that it does not exist at all, or will vanish
without a trace... The spirit is a truly free and intensive energy,
designed to contemplate the invisible, perceive the transcendent,
and concern itself with immortal elements, so as to come to an
understanding of its own calling and immortality through these very
concerns. It is pitiful that anyone would want to define the weakest
notion of the earthly world—the notion of death—as an immortal
and abiding state of the spirit...

There is a great Artist who created the external world, with
all of its magnificent laws and strict needs, and who has hitherto
continued to create the world of human souls with its marvelous
freedom and immortality. We are His sparks, His artistic creations,
His children. *We are immortal for this very reason.* And our earthly
death is nothing other than our metaphysical birth. It is true that a
person only rarely succeeds in acquiring his freedom in its entirety,
in the form of God's flame; only rarely does a person, in all of his
freedom, become a perfect artistic creation of the Spirit. But every

person has a certain level of that perfection within his reach. He matures his entire life as he approaches this upward step; during his entire life he *matures toward death*. And his earthly death comes upon him when he is not allowed to step up any farther, when he has nothing more to achieve, when he has matured enough for his departure in death.

My friend. It has been a great joy for me that I have been allowed to glimpse God's world, to hear its voice, perceive its living breath, however cursorily, sparingly, and helplessly. I always remembered that in addition to this grandeur (however brief and shallow my perception of it was) there is more: an endless wealth of beauty, majesty, and mysterious significance that I cannot perceive, which is lost to me. And yet—how wonderful that I was able even to visit this divine garden! How benevolent was the permission granted to me, how much did my spirit gain from this stay—from the delight of the flowers, from those joyfully radiant butterflies, from the silently prayerful mountains, from those streaming good tidings, from the quiet of the clouds, from that rejoicing of the birds, from every being born of earth. From the sea and the stars. From kind and wicked men, and especially from the great contemplatives who praised the Creator in word and thought, in song and painting, through depiction and study—and finally, directly through prayer. What undeserved wealth! What inexhaustible depth! It is truly a great gift that cannot be repaid...

And it was also a great joy to me that not only could I see this world, but also participate in its life with my life. I myself breathed, loved, and suffered; commited deeds and made mistakes; walked along the path of purification; believed and prayed; had the possibility of testing on myself the laws of worldwide existence and implementing my spiritual freedom through active decisions and deeds. I was offered the chance to live and mature toward death... Then I will be called away, since I have matured for this call, as if I have proven worthy to enter into communion with a new and previously unimaginable metaphysical wealth—in order to perceive it in a certain new, internal, and directly intimate manner. Everything I wasted and squandered, everything that I, as an earthly creature limited in my sensory perception, could not perceive and in which I dimly felt or blissfully sensed but could not describe in words the breath of my Creator—all of this and many other varied and wonderful things are awaiting me there, calling me there. All of this will be revealed to me anew in unearthly images and visions. Then I will perceive reality not as an object outside of me, but rather as a free and blessed joining to its real essence; this will be an artistic assimilation by which my spirit will be continually enriched, not so much losing its own shape as perfecting it. I still need the ability to see and understand everything, while remaining my own self; to perceive everything my earthly limitation kept from me; to experience in exultation all the miracles of God's wealth that have already been revealed to me (or have not yet been revealed to me) in the anticipation, dreams, and contemplations of my life on earth.

What awaits me is a long and blessed ascension to my Creator—to my Father, Savior, and Comforter—in awe and prayer, in purification and gratitude, in growth and confirmation. And therein lies the true meaning of my immortality, for any imperfection is unseemly to God and out of place in His creation.

That is how I understand the immortality of the human spirit.

V. AT THE GATES

God's Fabric

My neighbor came to visit me yesterday. He stayed for half an hour, puffing on his smoky pipe, and toward the end of the evening related to me what was foremost on his mind.

"My father, you know, was a very kind man. He died a long time ago, but when I think back on him my soul is filled with warmth and light. He was, you understand, a tailor, a good tailor, a master of his craft; he could put together a suit so well that it was a feast for the eyes. Dandies would come to us from neighboring cities and were always very satisfied; at first glance it was nothing special, but when you looked closer—well, it was simply a work of art. He always felt deeply for people. He would be sewing, singing a melancholy tune, and say suddenly: 'The neighbors treated Mitrevna badly yesterday, but they shouldn't have, they are all to blame,' or, 'Old Peter Sergeevich has nothing to wear for the holiday, he needs to have something,' and then keep sewing.

"Sometimes he would get excited and start to tell me about 'the fabric;' he never said 'material' or 'cloth,' but only 'fabric.' 'Look closely,' he would say, 'Nikolasha,[26] look at people. We are all cut from the same fabric. Here, look, each thread clings to the other and holds on to it; they are all intertwined, all evenly brought together.

---

[26] *Translator's note:* "Nikolasha" is a diminutive form of the name "Nicholas," used affectionately by the speaker's father in this story.

Just pull one thread out of this piece of cloth, and the entire fabric is ruined. If just one little thread is incompatible, if it frays, grows thin, or tears, the entire piece becomes defective. Not one skilled master would take such ailing fabric, not one customer would look twice at it. Therefore, go and look, and choose wisely, so that you don't make a mistake; I don't want any poor fabric in my factory."

"It is the same with people. Our God-given world is structured in such a way that we all are one continuous fabric. We cling to one another, hold each other, and hold onto each other. If anyone is unwell, the rest do not feel well. But people don't see this; they are foolish and near-sighted. They think, 'What do I have to do with him? I feel fine.' But that is not the case. If any one person feels unwell, then he suffers and is in pain; and his malaise radiates from him in every direction. He walks around with a gloomy aspect and makes others gloomy. Everyone feels ill at ease from his discomfort. Everyone becomes irritated at his anxiety. People's relations with one another turn sour: they don't trust each other, they suspect one another, offend each other, argue. And all of them feel that this stems from him, and for this reason they are irritated with him. He senses this and turns away from them, withdraws into himself, grows bitter. He needs love, but they treat him with annoyance. And no one sees his torment: they see only his gloominess, cruelty, and crossness, and they don't love him... And here is the rupture: the fabric has torn, it is being pulled in two, shredded apart. The hole must be quickly repaired, but no one takes it on himself to do this. 'What is it to me?' they ask. 'It is his concern, so he should be the one to repair it.' Meanwhile the tear grows and grows, and the fabric is ruined. Only love can repair it: your concerns are my concerns, our concerns are shared...

"Father would also say, 'It is the same with the economy. A poor man is not poor for himself, but for everyone. A beggar does not beg from himself; he troubles other people, speaks of his agony, bares his sores. Wherever there is sorrow, it is a *common* sorrow;

wherever there is hunger, the bread is bitter for everyone. The unemployed man does not wander about alone; we all suffer for him. It doesn't matter which tooth is aching—the entire person becomes distracted. An incompetent person, whether a failure or a drunkard, distributes his misfortune in all directions, touching everyone, burdening everyone. And again the entire fabric is ruined, and it must be repaired as soon as possible—everyone must help sew up the hole. If you cannot do it, *I* can do it for you; if neither of us can, then others will take it upon themselves.'

"He was the most kind-hearted of men, you know, my father. He helped everyone, anywhere he could. He would say, 'I was busy with some mending' or, 'I was darning a hole.' And so it was at times: he would gather the scraps from all the clothes and suits, or he would directly ask a customer for any remaining scrap and take it; he would twirl it around, turn it this way and that, put pieces together, adapt them, all very deftly... And then he would begin to sew. And in such cases he would sing happy tunes. You would look, and see he's made a vest or a pair of trousers. Sometimes he would even piece together an entire suit, wrap it up carefully in a scarf, and take it to a poor man. And he would forbid him to tell anyone. 'No one needs to know about this,' he would say. 'just keep quiet, that's all.' Only we in the family understood what was happening. But he was much beloved, to a rare extent. People came to him for advice, or just to cry on his shoulder.

"No, you know, he did not want to get rich; he would say there was no point to it. You will do fine supporting yourselves. What an inheritance... The things he said about fabric—that was our inheritance. When he felt his death draw near, he called me to him and said: 'I am going, Nikolasha. Do not grieve. We are all threads in God's fabric; and while we live on earth, it is our duty to preserve this fabric and strengthen it. Remember: the Savior had a robe, not sewn, whole, woven in one piece from top to bottom. We should remember this robe. We are its threads, and we are designed to be grafted into it after death. Remember it. This is the fabric of God. Keep it safe during your earthly life: strengthen every thread, guard it jealously with all your heart. Listen to your heart most of all. You must do what your heart whispers to you. And all will be well.'

"You know, it seems to me that he was right. We are all one fabric. In this, it seems to me, is hidden the wisdom of life..."

A Christmas Letter

This took place several years ago. Everyone was gathering to celebrate the Birth of Christ, decorating the Christmas tree and getting the presents ready. But I was alone in a strange country, with neither family nor friend; it seemed to me that I was forsaken and forgotten by everyone. I was surrounded by emptiness and felt no love: a distant city, strange people, callous hearts. And thus, in melancholy and despair, I remembered a collection of old letters which I had managed to preserve through the trials of our dark days. I took it out of my suitcase and found this letter.

It was a letter from my deceased mother, written twenty-seven years ago. What a joy that I had remembered it! Its contents are impossible to relate; the letter must be presented in its entirety.

"My dear child, Nikolenka,[27] you complain to me about your loneliness, but if you only knew how your words sadden and hurt me. If I could, with what joy would I come to you and convince you that you are not alone, nor can ever be alone. But you know that I can't abandon your father: he suffers much, and may need care at any moment. And you have to prepare for your exams and finish university. Well, let me at least tell you why I never feel loneliness. "You see, a man is alone only when he loves no one, because love is like a thread connecting us to a beloved person. We also create bouquets this way. People are flowers, and flowers that are gathered into a bouquet can never be lonely. As soon as a flower begins to

---

[27] *Translator's note:* "Nikolenka" is an affectionate form of the name "Nicholas."

really open and give off its fragrance, then the gardener will put it
into a bouquet.

"It is the same with people. A man who loves—his heart
blossoms and gives off fragrance; he gives his love just like the flower
gives off its scent. Then he is not alone, because his heart is with
those he loves: he thinks of them, cares for them, is joyful in their
joy and unhappy in their suffering. He doesn't even have time to feel
loneliness or to wonder if he is lonely. In love, a man forgets himself:
he lives with others, he lives in others. And that is true happiness.
"I can just see your inquiring blue eyes and hear your quiet objection
that this is only a *half-joy*—that complete joy is found not only in
loving, but also in being loved. But here is a little secret, which I will
whisper in your ear: he who truly loves does not demand or begrudge.
One should not constantly keep track and demand something in
return, wondering, 'What will my love give me? Will my love be
returned? Do I perhaps love more than I am loved? Is it even worth
giving myself completely to this love?'... All of this is untrue, and
unnecessary; it only means that love does not yet exist (it has not yet
been born), or exists no longer (it has died). This careful measuring
and weighing tears apart the living stream of love that pours forth
from the heart, and delays it. A man who measures and weighs does
not love. When he does so, an emptiness forms around him that
cannot be penetrated, cannot be warmed with the rays of his heart,
and others feel this right away. They sense it is empty, cold, and
hard around him; they turn away from him and expect to receive no
warmth from him. This makes him even colder, and thus he sits in
complete loneliness, forsaken and unhappy.

"No, my dear, love needs to flow freely from the heart, and
one shouldn't worry about it being mutual. One must wake people
up with love, one must love them and in this way call them to love.
To love is not a half-joy, but a *complete joy*. Simply accept this and
miracles will occur around you. Give yourself up to the current of
your heart, set your love free, let its rays shine and give off warmth

on all sides. Then you will soon feel the rays of reciprocated love flowing toward you from all around. Why? Because your immediate and unpremeditated kindness, your unceasing and selfless love, will imperceptibly draw kindness and love out of others.

"And then you will experience this reciprocal stream not as the complete joy that you demanded and sought, but rather as an *undeserved earthly blessing*, in which your heart will blossom and rejoice.

"Nikolenka, my child, think about this and remember my words as soon as you begin to feel lonely again. Especially once I am no longer on this earth. Be calm and full of good hope, because the Lord is our gardener, and our hearts are flowers in His garden.

"We both affectionately embrace you, Papa and I.
                                         Your mother."

Thank you, Mother! Thank you for your love and comfort. You know, I always finish reading your letter with tears in my eyes. And on that day, as soon as I finished reading it, the bells began to ring for the Christmas vigil service. Oh, what an undeserved earthly blessing!

A Wasted Day

Yesterday I had a wasted day. It seemed almost to happen by itself, but in the evening I sensed with my entire being that the day had been lost for me.

As soon as I woke up, I was attacked by various concerns. All kinds of mundane difficulties presented themselves, complications and even dangers, an entire nest of vipers. In vain I tried to free myself from them all with scorn and humor; in vain did I reproach myself for my timidity and pessimism; in vain did I seek solace in prayer. It was as if a crushing fog had descended upon my soul; the knots refused to disentangle, and my hopes were being extinguished. My imagination was conjuring up impending misfortune and wrongs, for when your life is governed by hard-hearted fanatics and spiritual fools, then you must prepare for anything. Bitterness and repulsion took hold of me. My heart convulsively shrank and hardened. I had to fight this. And that is how my wasted day began.

I had to gather all my strength and break down the walls, one after another. I had to find calm in my very anxiety, to concentrate, to weigh everything, to work out a plan and face the danger with dignity. I had to go on the offensive, to go from person to person, waking up my friends, convincing the obdurate, and expelling my enemies. I had to prove the indisputable, crush rocks, smelt metal... There are some happy people on earth who never even suspect what may become of life under the direction of heartless pedants—what deceit, what death, what desolation, what filth they bring to people, what we must go through because of them!

In the evening, after I came home and found that by some miracle all the knots had been untangled, I felt deathly tired. I had managed everything, my success exceeded all expectations, but the day was wasted.

It was wasted because my heart remained tremulously callous, and it had grown callous because I saw around myself the callous world and yet never noticed how it infected and poisoned me. When the heart grows callous, it is no longer capable of love: it does not sing or radiate; numbed and wounded, it becomes immersed in a dark silence; it has neither tenderness nor smile in it, and it is no longer capable of prayer. It turns to stone. And when the heart has turned to stone, then the person cannot be a divine instrument: so the day proves to be lost.

It was a lost day because I thought only about myself and bustled about for my sake alone. I had to find a way out of this impasse at which I found myself, and yet... Oh, that fear for one's own hide, as if it were so necessary and precious. Life begins to revolve around one's own self, as if there is nothing better or higher in heaven or on earth! Man becomes blind and deaf to the rest of the suffering world, and the living thread of God, which is the only thing worth living for on earth, seems to cease existing for him. And the day passes through his soul, dead and vulgar; it departs into the past like a flower that never bloomed.

This day was lost to me because I fought with people; because I tried to subjugate their wills to mine, to use them as my instruments; and because there was no living love for them in me—not for any one of them. I approached them carefully and cunningly, I persuaded them and tried to convince them, I imparted to them what I needed to, but I remained dry and matter-of-fact and just fixedly and watchfully observed them, like a stonemason looking over his clumsy bricks. What's more, they were repulsive to me, those cruel, self-satisfied, arrogant upstarts, and that repulsion reigned in my troubled soul. I had to hide this repulsion: to lie and be false, in loathing... Where can I place this burden now? How can I soften and wake up my heart? Will it awaken once more to love? ... Depart then, depart, lost day, so I can forget you completely and find healing.

Yes, the day was lost, because every beautiful and gentle thing on earth did not exist for me. The birds did not sing for me. The flowers did not gladden my heart or give off their fragrance for me. I did not see one child's smile. I did not dream at all of beauty. The cold wind swept over me as if I was a street lamp. I don't even remember if there was a sun in the sky yesterday. And even my innermost voice, which ever sings to me of distances and depths, grew silent, and its stream ran dry. The world as a gentle mystery, the world as a living anthem, the world as a miracle of God, did not exist for me. No, this was not life; I did not live that day.

It was dead to me because I did not find a single thread leading to the Kingdom of Heaven; not once did my gaze fix upon its wondrous, radiant fabric. On such days life is devoid of purpose or sanctity, no matter how lucky the person may be or how successful his worldly affairs. For man builds his life not through his affairs, but with his deeds; he breathes of preternatural currents; he lives for the rays approaching from a sacred distance; he lives by the breath of God...

Farewell, then, farewell, lost day. Vanish into oblivion.
I keep one single gift from you: I have seen your emptiness and
understood that you were a wasted day in my life…

About Patience

We all get the feeling from time to time that we are reaching the end
of our rope, that we can't go on, that "life is so difficult, so demeaning
and terrible, that I can't bear it any longer." But then time passes; it
brings us new burdens and new dangers, and we survive them; we
cope with them without becoming reconciled to them, and afterwards
have no idea how we were able to get through it or survive it all. The
illusion of "impossibility" dissipates the closer we get to the event;
the soul draws new strength from somewhere and we go on living,
only to fall prey again to that same illusion from time to time. This
much is clear: our gaze is near-sighted and our field of vision small;
we overlook our own strength—the strength that has been given to
us—and underestimate it. We don't know that we are much stronger
than we think, nor that we have a wonderful source which we fail
to cherish, wonderful abilities we never develop, a great force in our
individual and universal lives without which no culture could arise
or take root. I am referring to our *spiritual patience*.

What would become of us—and especially the Russian
people—if not for our spiritual patience? How would we manage
our lives and our suffering? All we need to do is glance over the past
thousand years in the history of Russia, and this question arises
naturally. How could the Russian people deal with those misfortunes,
deprivations, dangers, and illnesses, those trials, wars, and indignities?
How great was their endurance, their obstinacy, their loyalty and
devotion—their great skill at avoiding despair and persevering to the
end, rebuilding from ruins, rising from the ashes… And if we, the
late descendants of the great Russian "bearers" and patient ones, have
lost that skill, then we must rediscover it and restore it within ourselves.
Otherwise, there will be neither Russia nor Russian culture …

While life still goes on, it brings us its "yea" and its "nay"—strength and weakness, health and illness, success and failure, joy and grief, pleasure and revulsion. And so we must learn to calmly accept life's rejections as early as possible—to look the approaching "no" squarely in the eye and graciously greet the ungracious "underbelly" of our earthly existence. Let the low point of our lives come upon us, let the undesired, uncomfortable, repulsive, and terrible hang over us. We should neither consider flight nor curse our fate; on the contrary, we must think how to overcome our misfortune and how to defeat the enemy.

At first this may be both difficult and frightening, especially in childhood. How difficult a child's first loss is, how trying his first deprivations! Our first pain seems undeserved, and the first punishment excessively harsh... How easy it is for a child's soul to submit to jealousy, hatred, cruelty, or a sense of his own lack of worth! But all these injuries are essential and necessary in our lives for the development of our character. We must learn to endure without giving up, and grow accustomed to this. We must overcome our own cowardice and not give in to confusion. We must develop our life strategy: to calmly anticipate the advance of the "enemy" and greet success is impossible. The aptitude for spiritual success comes from extracting an increasing *renewal and revival of spiritual strength* from our battles with deprivations, dangers, and trials. Temptation is given us for the very purpose of creatively overcoming it—to cleanse us, make us deeper, more disciplined, stronger. And if happiness spoils and softens a person so much that he becomes weaker than his own self, then unhappiness educates him in *patience* and teaches him to be stronger than his own self.

And so first and foremost one needs the ability to overcome deprivations and disappointments, to welcome all dissatisfaction or unhappiness, and to courageously meet suffering with a "raised visor." This is not easy; one must study and teach oneself how to do it. Not everyone succeeds in this—and even then, not always, for it is natural for man to languish in a joyless life. Sometimes he may even be surrounded by impenetrable darkness, with no prospects or the smallest spark of hope. Then the steed of our instinct may rear up, displaying an indomitable stubbornness. For it is also in man's nature to seek comfort and entertainment; he is drawn to sensory pleasures, to strong and potent sensations; "hedonistic" by nature, he doesn't notice how much his own soul is gripped by desire and passions. He must know how to deal with any uprising of this natural hedonism. The answer is not to eradicate it from oneself; every creature needs his comfort, and man cannot live his life without happiness. The answer lies rather in ensuring that our *comforts do not depend on our external circumstances*; that our happiness has an internal source; that we may see light even where there is apparently nothing but impenetrable darkness. The revolt of our sensual nature must be conquered; otherwise, man risks demoralization. This sensual nature may be partially tamed through strength of will, or partially placated by new and different joys, or it may be exposed to an invocation of prayer: in each case, it is pacified.

In general, human life rests in self-direction and self-development, yet the art of living is the art of educating ourselves in the Divine. The more frightening and joyless our life, the more important it is to find perfection in the world and take unselfish pleasure in it. There is always a flower amid the grass, beauty in every cloud; every person has his own depth. Nature keeps silent about the eternal mystery; the starry sky speaks of detachment and eternity. Diversion, comfort, and joy await us at every turn; we need only the ability to perceive these qualities and give ourselves over to them. Sometimes it is enough merely to lift up our eyes to the heavens or glance at an icon written in inspiration. There is no joyless impasse in life that cannot be overcome with prayer, patience, or humor.

There are times when a person must be treated like a child. If, for example, a child grows weary of copying from a book, you must present him with a pretty new notebook in which to collect beautiful poems—and the joy of the activity will melt away the tediousness of the exercise. If it is boring for a child to repeat the covered material and eternally go back to the beginning, you must teach him how to blow soap bubbles. Let him find joy in the fleeting and fated beauty of the moment, let him achieve mastery of this innocent game and understand the purpose of effort and exercise for the sake of creation... We must carry out exercises patiently; we must introduce a competition for patience in our life; we must learn how to endure with ease. Let our children experience every joy and disappointment, all the pride and sense of power, that the school of patience gives us.

And whatever a person is made to bear—the din of machinery or a headache, hunger or fear, loneliness or anguish— he must from the start try not to fear, for a soul seized by fear loses We must not anticipate possible evils or give them shape in our imagination; if we do this, we make room for them in our lives prematurely, aiding them and rendering ourselves helpless. We intimidate and disappoint our patience, betraying it in advance.

Patience is, in its own way, *a trust in oneself and one's own strength*. It is *spiritual fearlessness*, tranquility, balance, presence of spirit. It is the ability to calmly and with dignity foresee the possible evil in one's life without exaggeration and to bolster one's own strength: "Let the unavoidable come—I am ready to manage and battle it, and I have the required stamina for it." We should not be scared for our own patience and consequently frighten it; nor should the craven words "I won't be able to stand it" ever appear in our soul. Patience requires us to trust ourselves; only then will it double and triple its efforts...

And if the hour has come, if the trial has begun and our patience has harnessed its strength, then it is important for us neither to doubt it nor question its stamina. It would be best not to think at all—neither of the fact that we are being patient, nor of our patience. But if we do think of our patience after all, we must do so with full confidence in its continuity. As soon as we say to ourselves, "Oh, I am suffering so much," or "I can't do it any more," matters immediately get worse. All we have to do is focus on our suffering, and it immediately begins to grow and inflate; it becomes an event in itself and overshadows all our spiritual perspectives. If we carefully examine our patience, we will suppress its direct and unnoticeable work: we observe it, subject it to doubt, and consequently render it powerless. Then, as soon as our patience ends, our impatience is immediately brought to light: the reluctance to endure, fight, or suffer; refusal; objection; weakness and despair. And when the soul is seized with despair, then the person is willing to do anything and is capable of anything, from shallow, demeaning compromise to the last base act. His case is closed and he is lost...

And what then? What is to be done? What should you do? At that point, it is better to fully purge your despair through tears, weeping, and grieving; you should open up to somebody, open your heart to a loyal friend. Or, better yet, you should vent your despair, your helplessness, and perhaps even your humiliation with words of utmost sincerity before the Father, who knows all secret things, and ask Him for strength from His Strength, comfort from the Comforter... Then the stream of your despair will run dry, the soul will be cleansed and your suffering comprehended, and the soul will again feel a blessed readiness to endure to the end, to victory.

However, it is better not to reach such a point of degradation and frustration. You must strengthen your patience so that it is not depleted. There are two approaches to this, two paths: *humor* in reference to yourself and *prayer* in turning to God.

Humor is a knowing smile at the sight of a suffering creature. This earthly wisdom assesses the creature's life according to the standards of the spirit, and sees its insignificance, its pretense, its blindness, and the comedy in it. This smile must arise from the suffering itself, it must be awakened in the creature's self-consciousness—only then will it provide true relief. Then patience itself will smile together with the spirit and the creature, and the person's entire soul will be united and confirmed in victory.

Prayer has the ability to lead a person away from suffering, elevating that person to Him who sent the suffering and thus called him to patience. Patience then participates in prayer; it ascends to its primary spiritual source and perceives its higher purpose. Nowhere can such serene patience be found as with God, who endures us together with our delusions, and unmatched is the sympathy for our suffering we find there, in the heavens. The human world is not alone in its suffering, for God suffers with it and for it. And that is why, when our patience concludes its prayer, it feels intoxicated by having drunk of the divine font. Then it realizes its true strength and knows that victory is at hand.

This is how the purpose of suffering and patience is revealed to us. We must not only accept and carry out the suffering sent to us, but we must also overcome it, i.e., be assured that *our spirit no longer depends on it*. Moreover, we must allow our suffering to teach us wisdom—natural wisdom and spiritual wisdom; it must arouse in us new sources of life and love; it must enlighten us anew as to the meaning of life.

Patience is in no way a passive weakness or a dull submission, as some believe; on the contrary, it is an *intensive activity of the spirit*. And the more it grips the purpose of the suffering that is being defeated, the stronger becomes its creative activity, the more assured its victory. Patience is not simply the art of waiting and suffering; it is also faith in victory and the path to victory; it is *the victory itself*, the conquering of weakness, deprivations, and suffering; it is victory over continuity, over boundaries, over time: the victory of man over his humanity and all his circumstances of life. Patience is truly "a ladder leading to perfection"...

And he who studies human history—he who sees how great was the suffering of men, and what came out of it—will come to know and recognize the great and fruitful power of patience. Upon it depends the staying power of every labor and creative act; it is the guide through every pitfall of temptation and suffering; it is the *instrument and force of Perfection itself*, battling for its realization in life. And for this reason it comprises the living foundation of the whole universe and every culture... Deprive a person of his patience, and everything—loyalty, modesty, humility; love, empathy, forgiveness; effort, courage, and works of research—will disintegrate into nothingness ...

Patiently, the caterpillar carries out its task—and transforms into a butterfly with beautiful wings. Man will develop wings even more beautiful if he lives and creates with true patience. For by drawing his strength from its supernatural source, he will be able to carry inhuman burdens and to create great and wonderful things on earth.

About the Conscience

There is an old legend about a kind king who lived in a certain land. Once upon a bitter winter evening, during a windy blizzard of blinding snow and snowy drifts, the king saw a poor man freezing on the road. His heart melted and, without thinking twice, he took off his warm mantle and wrapped it around the unfortunate man. "Let us go," he said to him, lifting him to his feet. "In my country a loving heart will be found even for you..."

Thus the conscience reveals itself in the human soul— often unexpectedly, but strongly and forcefully. No words are uttered, no commands. There is neither judgment nor formula in the consciousness. In wordless silence the conscience takes hold of our heart and our will. Its appearance can be compared to the ever-present but hidden force of power in an earthquake tremor. Words and thoughts come to us only later, in an effort to describe and explain the action we have committed.

In that instant when the conscience takes hold of our soul, we often get a feeling that something has awakened or arisen inside us—some special force that has apparently slumbered for a long time and has suddenly come to and powerfully turned over... This force lived inside me, but for some reason I never considered it my own, nor included it as part of me. That is to say, I do not know where it came from, yet it doesn't feel completely alien or foreign to me. It is as if it remained hidden somewhere inside of my very being, and I never thought it could prove so strong or reveal itself in such a way as it has just done. It seemed to me a mere *possibility* that has suddenly become a *necessity.* It was perceived as a distant call, but now has suddenly been discovered as wind and storm… It was like a pure spring of water breaking forth from the depths, which has suddenly turned into an unbridled, flooding torrent… At times it seemed to me that this was not a force, but rather a viable weakness—yet the moment of its power has suddenly arrived. More than once, I thought this was a beautiful but impossible dream of perfection in the world, and now suddenly this dream has become a life-affirming force…

In an instant, all sober conclusions and "intelligent" reasoning fell by the wayside; all my great passions and petty fancies grew silent; even my misgivings and fears vanished as if they never existed. I committed an action that I had never before committed; I had never even considered myself capable of it. But this action was solely correct and entirely right… Is it really true that I did it? Perhaps it wasn't I who did it, but someone else inside me. Someone better, bigger, braver and more just… But where did he come from? And where did he go? Will he perhaps appear again? Or was it I after all?

I know one thing for certain: I could not have acted otherwise. Something higher and stronger *compelled* me to act that way. It was as if something came over me, seized me, and carried me. As for any considerations of myself, my strength, or the consequences of my action, there was simply not enough time for that. And now, looking back, I admit that, strictly speaking, *I should not have dared* to act otherwise. I could not wish to do anything else, in that moment; and I will now say that I would not even want to have desired anything else, or to have acted otherwise. It was meant to be *so.* That was the best thing I could have done. And now, when I express all of these things, I feel a great and joyful inner certainty that I am speaking the simple truth. This certainty fills my heart and my entire being with a sort of calm, quiet bliss. I want only one thing: for *him*, that "better" and "bigger" person, to appear again, to perform his duty once more and again grant me this bright happiness...

So the conscience teaches a person to forget about himself and make his actions selfless. Sorrows, cares, misgivings, all the difficulties of his fate, are no longer ties that bind; all of this falls away, at least for a time, to the background. The person ceases to be an "individual" and suddenly becomes an object, in the best and most sacred sense of the word. This does not mean that he loses his persona and becomes "without person." No, the conscience confirms, builds, and strengthens a spiritually personal beginning in him. But the personally shallow, passionate, greedy, and wicked moves to one side and surrenders its place to the *breath of a higher life*, to the motivations and realities of the Kingdom of God, to objective reality described, strictly speaking, as "Ontological," or, with purer clarity, as "Objective." The person becomes like a living and joyful organ of the great and blessed Work, i.e., God's Work in the world. It is as if he had thrown off the burden of his selfishness, or suddenly grown wings which lifted him up and carried him out of the ravine of life. He committed his selfless act and returned, perhaps, to his gray, prosaic, everyday life, as if his wings have "fallen off" and he is once again fated to make his way in life on the streets of earthly greed... But he will never forget the feeling of blessed strength and freedom that he was allowed to experience. It visited him seemingly from another world, but he lived it, tried it, and will yearn for it forever.

We live on earth in a state of internal schism from which we suffer, but which we cannot overcome. This schism is a disparity between our personal, egotistical impulses and our *divine calling*, which we sometimes experience as an internal inclination, a spiritual thirst. We find ourselves in a state of spiritual division because the mysterious inclination to definitively and completely give in to God's

Work always exists in the depths of our heart. This inclination of the spirit always requires exactly the same thing of us: *the very best*. And if we gave in to it completely and conclusively, our entire life would be entirely made up of acts of love, courageous loyalty, the joyful fulfillment of duty, truth, and great service...

In reality, however, life goes otherwise: we hear this voice but fail to heed it—and when we do occasionally listen, our internal division deprives us of unity and doesn't allow us that great joy which exists in a unified soul. Then we perceive "submission" to our conscience as a dangerous life undertaking, an "adventure," an unreasonable and fanciful scheme; or, as Emmanuel Kant described it, as a joyless execution of duty and, consequently, an oppressive burden in life... However, even if we do not obey the voice of our conscience, a part of our being—and what's more, the better part—still remains committed to it, yet our internal division continues... Then, from the very depths of our spiritual core—whence the conscience initially calls out, whispers, weeps, sorrows, and rebukes—a discontent arises, a sadness and melancholy of a special nature, a tormenting disapproval. Sometimes we can successfully expel this oppressive but sacred disapproval from our conscience. In that case, the person finds a place for it in the deepest cavern of his soul, tries to lock up that vault and block the entrance to it. But this does not guarantee him freedom from the probable and even inescapable reproaches of his conscience, from that agonizing *gnawing* that will stay with him for the rest of his life, disrupting his spiritual balance and depriving him of spiritual peace.

Meanwhile, true healing, which promises unity of soul, needs only the person's assent, for only that assent can give him internal reconciliation and agreement between instinct and the spirit, the joy of willingness and objective service. I will be healed the moment I give in to the divine call of my conscience. Then I will do what *I am supposed to do*, but this will be neither an oppressive submission nor coerced penal servitude. Rather, it will be a bright joy in my life because I will be doing what my own will desires; and that which it desires will be *best thing*, and what's more, *truly* the best thing. And this best thing will become for me *an internal necessity*, the only possibility, an act committed, for I cannot act otherwise; I cannot desire otherwise; I do not desire the ability to do otherwise. Herein lies my duty, and I want to fulfill it not because it is my duty, but rather because it is the "objective best" to which my spirit (conscience) calls me, and to which my instinct also adheres with love. This is how a *conscience-driven unity* of the human soul is formed.

Before I knew what a "conscience" was, before I experienced the power and joy of the conscience-driven act, I used to ask in cold doubt: "Can it really be possible? Is man really capable of looking outside himself and suppressing in himself the healthy instinct of self-preservation?" Yet if I experience that conscience-driven act even once, profound changes come about. All my old doubts and skeptical questions fall away; denial and irony cease to exist. I know that this conscience-driven act is possible, because I myself experienced it in reality. True, I don't know if, when, or under what circumstances it will be repeated. But who can prevent me from *calling out to my conscience* on my own initiative? Why must I think that it will not answer my call? And when it answers, I can freely and joyfully surrender to its summons. All of this is in my power, and all will take place in my internal world... All I need to know is how best to do this so as not to replace the voice of my conscience, to fall into delusion, error, or self-deceit...

First of all, I must put aside every theoretical intellectualiza-tion, for it will invariably bring with it the formation of thoughts, assessments, analysis, and synthesis, cloaking everything with concepts and words. None of this is necessary, for an act of the conscience is not an act of *worded thinking*: it is neither theory nor doctrine, nor a "maxim," nor a law or norm. I need not compose anything; I do not need to contemplate or contrive anything. I need not strive toward some sort of "universal legislation." I don't need to *anticipate anything*. I only need await that certain, emotionally driven underground tremor.

Nor must I ask what would be the "most useful" or "most advisable" thing; these questions are decided by life experience, observation, and reasoning. Even more so, I should never ask what would be the "pleasant," "comfortable," "advantageous," "smart," etc., thing to do; none of this has any connection to the conscience-driven act. I have to seek the best, the *morally best* thing, and furthermore not merely the best thing according to me, but truly *the best thing.* The believing Christian will ask about "the most Christian thing," the most ideal thing from the viewpoint of Christ the Savior.

And another thing: this question should not be posed theoretically, with the aim of discovering, getting to know the truth, formulating and proving it; that would be nothing more than philosophical study, contemplation, and theoretical examination. The question should be given *practically* in order to do, to act, to realize. And since every practical case in life is individual and unique in its kind, then I must seek in any given real-life situation not some general rule, but an individual indication of an individual action.

And so without any preconceived decisions—without any stipulations, "conditions," evasions, or "reservations"—I will stand up as I am before my conscience, in the given specific moment of my personal life, in the "here" and "now," to heed its voice, to answer its call, and to commit an act from the depth of my heart. I will ask how I should act in order to realize here and now the most Christian thing, the most ideal thing in the sight of Christ the Savior.

I pose the question—and release it into the open depths of my heart. And life goes on. Then the desire is given on its own. The deadened heart awakens, and...the king's mantle is placed on the shoulders of the poor man...

The king's mantle? Yes I, with my deadened heart and callous nature, am like the poor man sitting by the road of life, covered by the snowstorm of daily cares and reckonings. The Lord found me, freezing and half-dead; He leaned down to me, clothing me with His Garment, as light, as love, as revelation. And in the act of the conscience, man receives from God this revelation, love, and the light of a new life.

About Optimism

Healthy, constructive optimism: this is vital for contemporary mankind like air, like fire and water. We stand on the brink of a new era, and we need new creative ideas; we must look at once into the depths and into the distance; we must want what is true, desiring it with a strong will; and to crown all, we must believe that future renewal is within our grasp. We must approach the resolution of impending tasks with dignity and calmness, and simultaneously with great, creative concentration, for the development of the world's history depends on our success. Huge efforts will be required of us in every sphere of life, for this is a matter of religious, cultural, social, and political renewal.

And for this, *spiritually faithful optimism* is irreplaceable.

However, we also come across a false, deceitful optimism in life. It is not enough to be "in a good mood" and insufficient to not anticipate anything bad. The frivolous merry-maker is always in a good mood, while the near-sighted and naïve man will not anticipate anything at all. It is not enough to believe in our own strength and to have the ability to calm other people; self-confidence can hinder the artistic process, and optimism does not amount to "calmness," by any means. Optimism is not given to people from birth, or as a result of good health; it is acquired in spiritual maturity. The optimist does not foresee success and happiness under every condition: the progression of history may portend not a rise, but a fall, and the optimist cannot close his eyes to this. But he remains an optimist, all the same.

And so, there is *false optimism* and spiritually faithful optimism.

The false optimist maintains his good mood because he is a man of moods and is affected by personal, purely subjective conditions. His "optimism" does not have any objective grounds. He lives on his own terms, outside of the profound passages of history, outside of the world's great events. He is an optimist only because he boasts a healthy, balanced organism and doesn't suffer from spiritual disharmony. His "optimism" pertains to himself and maybe his personal matters. But in the plane of great achievement he sees little, or perhaps nothing, even; and if he really does see something, he sees it dimly and assesses it incorrectly. When faced with spiritual problems, he is superficial and flippant; he perceives neither their depth nor their scope, and then matter-of-factly accepts his shallow visions as genuine reality. This is why he sees neither God's emanations nor His signs. And that is why his "optimism," while physiologically explainable and spiritually motivated, is objectively and metaphysically ungrounded; and he takes no responsibility for it. His optimism is the manifestation of his personal daydreaming, or even his arrogance; it can lead to veritable absurdity, and his confident grandiloquence carries no more weight than the chirping of a grasshopper...

The situation is entirely different in the soul of the true optimist. First of all, his optimism does not pertain to mundane existence with all its tangles, alleyways, and dusty trivialities, all of its cruelty and viciousness. Everyday life can overwhelm us with its increasingly frightening burdens, deprivations, and suffering, but this does not affect his optimism in any way, for he views these trials as steps preparing him for deliverance. He keeps in mind the *spiritual problem* of humankind, the fate of the world, and understands that this fate is conducted and resolved by *God Himself*, that it unfolds like a great and creative living drama. This is the true and deepest source of his optimism: he knows that *the world rests in the hollow of God's Hand*. He tries to perceive the unmistakable, creative activity of this Hand—not merely in order to understand it, but to willingly place himself, as a free agent, at the mercy of that good and sublime Hand ("Thy will be done"). He desires to participate in God's Work and plan, yearns to serve and lead, heed and create: he desires whatever corresponds to the will of God, His plan, His idea. He sees how a sort of divine tapestry is created and woven in the world, the living tapestry of the Kingdom of God; he foresees the image of this tapestry and rejoices at the thought that he also will be able to enter it with his living thread.

This means that his optimism relates less to human concerns than to God's Work. He believes in a bright future, in the approaching Kingdom, because it cannot help but come, for it is realized by God. And his main goal is to faithfully perceive the place assigned him and to faithfully perform the service predestined for him.

Having once discovered his place in God's plan and having found his true service, he strives to better realize his calling—to execute his "optimism." And if he knows that he is doing this, then a quiet *joie-de-vivre* and a spiritual optimism descends upon him. He believes in his calling and his Work. He looks upon himself as a thread in God's Hand; he knows that this thread is woven into God's tapestry of the world, and thus he feels that he is preserved under God's protection. He goes forth with prayer to meet the unavoidable dangers of life and calmly tramples underfoot "the lion and adder, the young lion and the dragon" (Psalm 91) while remaining unharmed; and for this reason he confesses together with Socrates that no harm can befall a servant of God...

This means that the true optimist never overestimates his personal strength. He is no more than one of the mortal threads in the Hand of the great Creator of life, and this mortal thread can be cut at any moment. But while this thread remains on earth, it desires to grow stronger and to serve faithfully. Such a man is governed by a will for dedication and victory. And whereas the pessimist completely shuts down his will and finds himself lost amid events, whereas the false optimist gives in to his moods and doesn't deal with complications, the true optimist copes with any task. He keeps a keen and sober eye on all events without giving in to fear, or exaggerating the dangers; the more accurately he sees reality, the better he understands how much strength of will and endurance is required of him. He is a strong-willed person who is conscious of being watched over and preserved, dedicated to that Work which he serves, taking nourishment from the Divine Font for the internal stream of his will for life.

For the will is a wonderful and mysterious force that can always become more powerful and stubborn than it may seem at first. The true optimist's will is a *gift of strength*, the art of self-strengthening, a living continuity of effort: the spiritual *perpetuum mobile* (perpetual motion) hopelessly sought so long ago...

The true optimist sees the passage of his contemporary history, contemplates its existence and purpose in God's plan, and draws his strength from the endless source of his will, which is dedicated to and acknowledged by God. He unwaveringly believes in the victory of his Work—even though this victory may be viewed by the ages as his personal defeat, for his victory is the doing of God Whom he serves on earth. And when he is overtaken by fatigue or uncertainty, then he prayerfully calls to the ultimate source of his will and his life—to God.

Then he is given everything he needs, and he continues his service.

About Sincerity

While man lives on earth, he remains alone; he is not given the freedom to break out of this loneliness or to remove it completely. The primary method of existence inherent in man remains eternally the same and does not change for thousands of years. And if it did change its very nature, then man would cease to be himself; he would become a kind of "super-human" or something "not-quite-human," of which we have not the slightest notion.

Each of us has a unique soul that is closed off within itself, hidden within a unique and one-of-a-kind individual body with which it is mysteriously connected, and which serves it and expresses its varied states of being. This method of existence provides us with all the burdens and gracious benefits of the isolated life.

Isolation[28] is a burden, for it would be much easier to become lost in the cohesive and dependent existence of other people—to drown in total assimilation, rather than to confirm our *singularity and independence* or, what's more, to confirm it to the appropriate extent, i.e., to go through life alone, taking the responsible, sincere, and creative path. Yet loneliness also has its great and beneficial advantages, because it is a living foundation and essential prerequisite of *freedom of spirituality, personal purification, and enlightenment.*

Life would be terrible if man had no internal aloofness, if he had no chance of withdrawing into a chaste and guarded isolation in order to concentrate on himself, to find himself and to work on his purification and self-perfection. In such a case, man would be like a house with transparent walls, where everything could be seen from the outside, or like a public house, constantly and completely open to vermin, animal, and villain. There would be nothing hidden in his life, nothing guarded, untouched, or sacred, only a draft blowing unchecked; people eternally passing through and breaking in; a sidewalk, open for every abuse. A faceless and shapeless assimilation. An eternally trampled-upon relic...

What a wonder, what a wise arrangement it is that we, thanks to our human way of living on earth, are protected from such mutual intrusion, profanation, and outrage. What beneficial and even blessed meaning is hidden in our earthly "shell," our body: it protects the impenetrability of our soul, it defends our spirit's self-realization,

---

[28] We must distinguish between "loneliness" and "isolation." A person's loneliness means that he has little connection with others; little interaction; little mutual understanding, sympathy, friendship, and love. This is juxtaposed with non-loneliness, i.e. a rich and varied social interaction and an abundance of creative ties with others. This is realized within the boundaries of that universal trait, isolation, because both scarcity of social ties and wealth of social interaction are defined by and exist within the boundaries of man's inescapable, and necessary for his survival, isolation. Isolation is a method of existence, present both in the misunderstood man living in seclusion and the successfully social, varied in companions, individual. All are lonely through their isolation. But the latter kind fills his isolation with a generous and blossoming interaction with others, thereby noticing it less and suffering from it less. The former kind gives in to his loneliness within the boundaries of his isolation, and he is specifically able to explore its essence, its spiritual purpose, and its rules, to the very core.

it watches over the mystery of our personal interaction with God and the journey toward Him. Man is appointed thus "from nature" so that he may remain *alone with God*; and he was created as such so that the Lord may be *alone with him*. Man is an individual creative center, for in him is laid that firm boundary, that restraint, by which any willful, anti-religious, collectivized body which is contrary to nature will be defeated…

However, man's isolation and independence was not given only for the purpose of separating him from his neighbors, or to turn him into a sly schemer, a universal deceiver… A person's self-identity and originality (let's call it his "self-capacity") by no means constitutes a rejection of interaction, mutual dependence, or love. Spiritual "autocracy" (absolute rule) need not lead to arrogance or pride. Detachment is given to a person so that he may freely turn to God, purifying and strengthening himself in His Spirit, and thus enter into communion with others *as a son of Love*—free, yet rooted in God. Individuality is given to man as a means to the free contemplation of God, as the possibility to become a spirit, to lead a spiritual life and create a spiritual culture. In this lies the goal of his life; this is what he was designed to create and develop with himself.

Man is a world on a smaller scale, a microcosm, and he must realize in himself, and in relation to himself, spiritualization, purification, and management. In other words, he must build his spiritual character with the intention of subsequently including himself and creatively inserting himself into the larger world: the macrocosm. A person's independence is not his right to despotism or atrocity. His freedom should not be interpreted as freedom *from* the spirit, from the conscience, from religion. On the contrary, the world's great symphony requires us to strengthen and encourage within ourselves our own independent voice and to unite our free, individual song to the true harmony, the universal chorus, thus achieving God's predestined worldwide rhythm.

And so man's loneliness is a high and difficult skill, while *sincerity* is its best manifestation.

In order to be sincere, a person must internally discover himself and have sufficient courage to remain true to himself. To discover himself means to perceive with the heart his own sanctity and to grow attached to it, to submit his life to it. Until the person has done this, he will waver between the various possibilities that appeal to him, place claims on him, or tempt him. Not one of them, however, has the absolute advantage over the others; not one is definitive, and so he can give in to them and play with every one in turn. His heart belongs to "nothing," and so at any moment he can change and make changes, begin to "feel" differently, betray any cause. His spirit, as a thing belonging to no one (*res nullius*), will belong to the first claimant (*primo occupanti*), as the Roman humorists said. Such a man treats nothing seriously or reverently. There is not a single opportunity for him in life which is the "only" possibility, i.e. the most important and essential thing. He doesn't even understand how it can be *essential* to be "so," and *only* so, to act "so" and *only* so....

A man becomes sincere when there is a certain *sacred concentration* in his soul, which he regards with serious and complete reverence—when he *cannot and does not want* to do otherwise in his life choices and actions. Then he stands firm; then he has a strong anchor, or a mighty and living root. Then he *cannot* want anything else, nor would he want to be able to do otherwise. And then all he needs is the courage to stay faithful to his sanctity and to derive from it everything in his life.

In order to be sincere, a person must become *internally unified.* While his spirit remains fragmented or torn apart, he neither loves, thinks, speaks, nor acts sincerely. A civil war rages within him; he simultaneously pursues different goals and serves different values ("gods"); several life "centers" compete within him—and he betrays each one for the next. Everything in him is duplicitous and untrue; his love is not strong and is worth little; his thinking is conditional and relative; he wanders and doubts, and creates nothing; his words are false; in decisions he remains always calculating; in deeds he is unreliable, and he knows no loyalty. He therefore has a weak

character, and is not dependable. The first and most basic rule of
"individuality" is the rule of *internal indivisibility*, but he does not
observe this rule; he does not live by it. Thus he is always insincere,
even when he is on his own, when he thinks to himself and makes
"lonely" decisions. For he has no internal cohesion—and without it,
he has no sincerity either.

A man is sincere when he carries in himself a central flame
from which light spills forth, and from which sparks fly in all
directions.

The ancient Greeks and Romans had a holy shrine in every
house, on which readily smoldering coals always lay. This shrine
was called Hestia (Ἑστία) in Greek and Vesta in Latin, and it was
venerated as the holy center of the home.

The Pythagoreans insisted that the world has a great central
fire (Κέντρον, Μέσον), a firstborn sacred flame which is the creative
source of light, warmth, and order. Philolaus designated this center
with the word Hestia: it was at the same time the "House of God"
and the connecting force of everything, and a creative source of nature's order. From this source stemmed the heartbeat of the world...

And so every one of us is called upon to confirm in ourselves
this shining and governing *burning bush* and to live in its light and
law. He who allows his life to proceed from this center becomes
sincere. His Hestia illuminates all of his work, and he himself emits
her rays into his life. She gives him warmth and energy, and his heart
becomes a Bush and shines upon other people. His entire life receives
direction and guidance from this Bush; from this rhythm his life
becomes whole and centralized, and his own will becomes true and
strong. Then all the sparks of his love, his thoughts, and his actions
fly out from this flame. The Bush in his heart sends him *its* words,
and they become *his* words; his decisions and views, the letters and
books that he writes, all become sincere; his very soul proves bright,
light, determined, and sincere.

Sincerity is courage, so man also becomes courageous. Sincerity is *devotion to truth*, and so man becomes a true champion of God's work. Sincerity is the transparency of a burning soul; similarly, man becomes flaming and transparent. All this means that he has happily resolved the problem of detachment and has succeeded in *the art of loneliness...*

Such people are destined to execute the most important things in life, culture, and history: their work is prayer and sanctification, contemplation and knowledge, education and spiritual nourishment, academia and art, government and judgment. They are given true friendship in life, which springs from a creative exchange of sparks. Such people are the pillars of the church, the family, and government, for all human unions degenerate in the absence of spiritual sincerity, in lies and deceit, in falseness and betrayal. Only sincerity renders them viable and strong.

A church that is built on insincerity and enslaved to insincerity distorts and perverts the matter of religion; it has lost the door leading to the Kingdom of Heaven; it has installed falsehood in a holy place, it is an *imaginary* church. A family built on pretense and deceit is an empty illusion: it produces interactions filled with deceit and an imaginary unity; it has no spiritual power and is doomed to fall apart. A government founded on lies and built on violence, fear, and hypocrisy is organized depravity: it undermines and extinguishes mutual trust; it perverts and weakens the individual's conscience and honor; it deprives human life of its divine purpose and its creative freedom.

And yet there is a noble and blessed force in human life that cannot exist without sincerity, and always achieves it. This is the power of the *living heart*. The heart can only love sincerely; insincere love is not love at all. The heart can only sing sincerely; the discordant song of a false heart does not ring true before God. The heart can pray only sincerely; prayer that does not arise from the Bush of the heart is the foreshadowing of an incomplete prayer, or simple hypocrisy. Insincere faith is self-deceit and simulation. Insincere art is false and inartistic. Insincere kindness is repulsive duplicity.

Modern man's great misfortune lies is the fact that he has lost all sincerity of heart. His salvation can only be found in its restoration and in the subsequent creation of a new culture. Anything that delays this process of healing and renewal can only be harmful. Most harmful of all, most pernicious of all, is that which suppresses and weakens, shatters and undermines, the sincerity of the human heart.

What can a man undertake or create with a deadened heart, when everything great and profound, everything divine in life, requires sincerity and love? Nothing great or enduring has ever arisen out of duplicity and deceit. That is why sincerity is a gift from God and man's treasure. And if modern mankind wants to be healed and reborn, then it must return to the strength and joy of the sincere heart.

EPILOGUE

The Singing Heart

There is only one true joy on this earth: *the singing of the human heart.* If the heart sings, the person has almost everything—almost, because he still must save his heart from becoming disillusioned in a beloved subject and falling silent.

The heart sings when it loves; it sings from love, which flows in a living stream out of a certain mysterious depth and never runs dry, even when suffering and torment come upon it, or when the person is overtaken by misfortune, or when his death draws near, or when an evil undertaking in the world celebrates its victory and it seems that the power of kindness has dried up and been condemned to death. If the heart still sings in spite of all this, then the person has true "happiness," which, strictly speaking, deserves a different, better name. Then the rest of his life seems less important; then the sun never sets, God's rays do not forsake the soul, the Kingdom of Heaven enters life on earth, and life remains blessed and transformed. And this means that *a new life* has begun, that the person has embarked upon a *new existence.*

We have all experienced a dim reflection of this happiness—for example, when we were completely and tenderly in love. However, that was really nothing more than its reflection, or a faint foretaste. Many experience even less than that, only a distant hint of a premonition of a great possibility... Of course, the heart that is completely and tenderly in love, like that of Dante, Petrarch, or Pushkin, feels enthralled, full, and overflowing; it begins to sing, and when its song is successful it brings people light and joy. But this is given only to a gifted minority capable of singing sincerely out of a pure heart. Typical earthly lovesickness makes the heart suffer, or even feel ill, heavy, and obscured; it often deprives the heart of its purity, lightness, and inspiration. The soul, agitated and intoxicated with passion, does not sing but rather sighs and moans helplessly; it becomes greedy and particular, demanding and blind, envious and jealous. The singing heart, on the other hand, can be benevolent and generous, happy and forgiving, light, clear, and inspired. Earthly lovesickness binds and attaches; it drives the heart into a ravine of personal worries and renders it egotistical. But true love accomplishes the opposite: it liberates the heart and guides it toward the great scope of God's world. Earthly lovesickness extinguishes itself and ceases to exist in the sensory fulfillment through which it is enervated and disappointed. The intoxication passes, the soul sobers, the illusions dissipate, and the heart grows silent without having sung a single hymn. Often, too often, the enamored heart sighs fruitlessly, sighs and beats, thirsts and groans, spills tears and cries out—but it does not understand its fate, does not comprehend that its happiness is deceptive, transient, and meager, no more than a reflection of true bliss. And the heart loses that spark without learning either song or contemplation, without experiencing either happiness or love, without beginning its enlightenment or gracing God's world.

* * *

The heart sings not from lovesickness, but out of love; its song pours forth in endless melody, with an eternally living rhythm, eternally novel harmonies and tones. The heart acquires this ability only when it allows itself access to the divine elements of life, leading its depth into a living communion with the non-disillusioning treasures of heaven and earth.

Then begins true singing, which neither ceases nor runs dry, because it flows from an eternally self-renewing happiness. The heart sees the Divine in everything, rejoicing and singing; it shines from that depth where the person's individuality merges with the transcendently divine to the point of becoming indistinguishable, for God's rays pierce through the person, and the person becomes God's beacon. Then the heart inhales love from God's expanse and gives love of its own accord to every creature, every dusty speck of existence, and even to the evil person. Then the sacred blood of Existence flows and pulsates through him. Then the breath of God breathes within him…

Somewhere in the most intimate depths of the human heart slumbers a certain spiritual eye, designed to contemplate the divine elements of heaven and earth. This mysterious eye, with all of its receptivity and power of sight, must be roused inside a person in his earliest and most tender childhood if it is to awake from its primeval sleep, to open and gaze into the divinely created vastness of being with a blessed and insatiable thirst for contemplation. This eye, having once awakened and opened, is like an exposed emotional core that forever remains accessible to everything that guards God's flame within itself; it perceives every spark of living perfection, takes joy in it, loves it, enters into a living connection with it, and calls the person to dedicate his personal strength in service to God's Work.

The ancient Greeks believed that the gods had a certain divine drink called "nectar" and a divine food called "ambrosia." And it is true: there really is such spiritual sustenance, but it is intended for people, rather than the gods of Olympus. The hearts of those who taste of it begin to sing.

The heart sings upon contemplating of nature, for within it everything shines and glistens from those "sparks of living perfection," like the sky on an August night. The heart also sings from its contact with people, for in every one of them lives a divine spark, flaming forth and conquering, beckoning, shining, forming the soul spiritually and calling out to other sparks. The heart sings, perceiving the mature creations and heroic acts of the human spirit—in art, in knowledge, in virtues, in politics, in rights, in labor, in prayer—for every one of these creations and acts is the living incarnation in man of God's will and God's law. But most wonderful of all is the song that pours forth from the human heart towards the Lord in His grace, His wisdom, and His majesty. And this song, full of anticipation, blessed contemplation, and grateful, unspoken trepidation, is the beginning of that new existence and the manifestation of that new life...

* * *

Once, during my childhood, I saw little particles of earth's dust playing and exulting in a ray of sunshine. They fluttered and spun round, vanished and swam out once more, darkened in the shadows and grew bright again in the sun. I understood then that the sun can treasure, adorn, and gladden each little speck of dust, and my heart sang out in joy...

One warm summer day, I lay down in the grass and saw a world hidden from the ordinary eye, full of beautiful peculiarities; a wonderful world of light and shadow, living communion and joyful growth; and my heart sang out, wondering and marveling...

I used to sit for hours on the shores of the mysterious, menacing, and beautiful Black Sea in Crimea, listening to the babbling of its waves, the rustle of its pebbles, the call of its gulls, and the sudden crowning silence. And I tremulously thanked God with a singing heart...

One time I was able to contemplate a white peacock's dance of love. I stood in awe of its most elegant fan of lace, gracefully unfolded and trembling in concentration, of that combination of haughty grace and loving veneration, of the playful gravity of its light and energetic movements; I saw purity, beauty, and the sinlessness of love in nature—and my heart bloomed in joy and gratitude...

At sunset, in the gentle radiance and deep, half-sleeping silence, our ship sailed into the Corinth Canal. The distant mountain chain slept in rosy light; the steep banks of the canal towered like a stern guard; people and birds remained reverently quiet, watching and hoping… And suddenly the banks parted before us, the milky-green Adriatic waters carrying us flooded into the dark blue bosom of the Aegean Sea—and sun and water met us with the exulting of light. Can I ever forget that joy, when my heart will always answer it with exulting song?

Every heart blooms and sings at the sight of the trusting, affectionate, and helpless smile of a child. Can it be otherwise?

Every one of us feels the gathering tears in the eye of our heart when we see true human kindness, or hear the timid and tender song of another's love.

Every one of us takes part in a higher, sublime joy when we heed the voice of our conscience and give in to its flowing stream, for this stream already sings an exultant melody of the successful victory of the world hereafter.

Our heart sings when we bury a hero who has served God's Work on earth.

Our heart sings when we contemplate true sanctity in a painting, when we perceive spiritual light through the melody of worldly music, hear in it the voices of singing and prophesying angels.

Our heart sings at the sight of the mysteries, miracles, and beauty of God's world; when we contemplate the starry sky and perceive the universe like a harmonious summation; when human history reveals to us the sacred mystery of Providence and we see the passage of God through ages of trials, labor, suffering, and inspiration; when we are present at the victory of a great and just cause.

Our heart always sings in times of total and inspired prayer…

* * *

And if we are given, in addition to this, the opportunity to participate in and to influence world events with a measure of love, then our happiness in life may be complete. For we can be truly certain that in the development of this world nothing passes without a trace, nothing is lost, nothing vanishes: not one word, one smile, or one sigh… He who even once made another heart happy has bettered the entire world as a result; he who knows how to love and to gladden others becomes an artist of life. Every divine moment of life, every sound of the singing heart, influences world history more than those "great" events, economies, and politics which exist in the flat and cruel plan of earthly life and whose aim often lies in acquainting people with their vulgarity and their mortality.

We must recognize and accept that those divine moments of life constitute the *true substance of the world*—that a person with a singing heart is God's island, His beacon, His ambassador.

And so there is only one true joy on this earth, and that joy is the bliss of the loving and singing heart, for it grows into the spiritual substance of the world while it yet lives and thus partakes of the Kingdom of Heaven.

About the Translator

A lexandra Weber (née Kotar) is a literary translator, lifetime student of Russian cultural history, Marine Corps wife, and Orthodox Christian. She holds a Bachelor's degree in English Language and Writing from the University of San Francisco and a Master's degree in Russian Literary Translation from Columbia University. At Columbia, her research interests included the cultural legacy of the first wave of Russian emigration to Europe and Asia during the early-twentieth century. Her main work involved the translation of personal memoirs written during the Soviet Era, both in Russia and in the Diaspora. She also worked at Columbia's Bakhmeteff Archive, processing such collections as the papers of Russian émigré activist Alexander Kazem-Bek. In addition to her ongoing translation projects, Alexandra loves to travel, and dreams of pursuing her research of the Russian emigration's cultural history in every new place she visits.

About the Orthodox Christian Translation Society

The Orthodox Christian Translation Society (OCTS), a Pan-Orthodox non-profit organization, is an international publishing house exclusively dedicated to producing translations of Orthodox texts of unsurpassed quality in languages around the world. Since Pentecost, overcoming language barriers has been an essential part of God's work through His saints. OCTS continues the work begun at Pentecost by supporting the translation of Orthodox texts so that people of every tongue can be inspired by the words of our holy fathers and mothers in the faith regardless of their background. OCTS believes in the unique value of translation for the spiritual edification of the Orthodox Church worldwide.

The mission of OCTS begins with highly qualified Orthodox Christian translators who submit their proposals to translate texts that they believe would be of great benefit in the target language. OCTS chooses proposals to fund based on several criteria, including the competence of the translator, the relevance and importance of the text, the achievability of the project, and the marketability of the final publication. The OCTS Advisory Board affirms which projects they believe would be of the most spiritual benefit. OCTS commits to financially support chosen projects from the first draft of translation all the way through the editing, publication, and distribution of the finished project. OCTS raises funds through grants and donations, invests the proceeds from the sale of our publications back into the organization, and hopes to provide a source of reliable, edifying, and relevant translations for generations.

Made in United States
Troutdale, OR
11/10/2024

24606025R10116